Christians
Single, *Again!*

A Seeker's Guide to Biblical Marriage
For Those Divorced or Remarried

⚜

Gresham R. Holton, *Ph.D.*

Published by

Growing Panes

3543 Raintree Drive - Valdosta, Georgia 31601

Gresham R. Holton

Christians
Single, *Again!*

A Seeker's Guide to Biblical Marriage
For those Divorced or Remarried

GROWING PANES, INC.
3543 Raintree Drive * Valdosta, GA 31601

Copyright © 2014 Gresham R. Holton
grholton@yahoo.com

ISBN: 0990549909
ISBN-13: 978-0-9905499-0-1

Scripture taken from the New King James Version®. Copyright © 1982 by Thomas Nelson. Used by permission.

Printed by CreateSpace, An Amazon.com Company
Available from Amazon.com, CreateSpace.com, and other retail out
2014

CONTENTS

Chapter 1: SINGLE-AGAIN

- Learning to "Live Single"
- Biblical "Super-Saints"?
- Threat of Sexual Immorality?

Chapter 2 : MARRIAGE

- Defining the "Ideal" Marriage?
- Roles in the Marriage?
- A "Sacred Sexual Partnership"
- Boundaries of Commitment

Chapter 3: MAN AND WOMAN

- The Promises of Love

- Vows of Faithfulness
- Two become One
- Marital Intimacy: A Spiritual Partnership

Chapter 4: BIBLICAL MARRIAGE

- Creation: God's Image on Display
- Children: Replenishing God's Image
- Character: Creating Unity in Diversity
- Christ: The Ideal Image of God
- The Ideal Biblical Marriage Model
- Marriage Corrupted by Sin

Chapter 5: DIVORCE

- Divorce: It's Really Bad
- Divorce: What happened!?
- Common Sins of Marriage
- Divorce? No! God hates it!

Chapter 6: DIVORCE

- "*Allowable*" Grounds for Divorce
- Divorce for Sexual Immorality Only
- Divorce for Desertion
- Divorce for Abuse and Neglect
- Divorce for Covenant-breaking
- The "Pauline Privilege" Principles

Chapter 7: FORGIVENESS

Chapter 8 – SPIRITUAL RECOVERY

Chapter 9: RESTORING FAITHFULNESS

Chapter 10: REMARRIAGE

Gresham R. Holton

Dedicated

To my wife,

SHARLENE

My best friend for more than 60 years and loving partner

in our spiritual journey of biblical marriage

Gresham R. Holton

FOREWORD

Divorce is a painful but inescapable reality in modern America. Few families in our nation have completely escaped the sad consequences of broken marriage vows, broken dreams, and broken relationships. As millions of Americans face the stark reality of divorce, they turn for assistance and guidance to counselors and to lawyers, as well as family, friends, and the church. Most are seeking understanding, compassion, healing, and direction for their lives. Sadly, many sufferers find none of these when they turn to their family and friends for help. Like the woman in John 8 who was brought before Jesus after getting caught in an adulterous situation – they felt like those closest to them were ready to throw their individual stones at the divorcee and to leave them for dead.

Many who pass through divorce find themselves even more deeply estranged from their churches! All too often, when they turn to church leaders or members of their congregation for spiritual assistance, they are met with embarrassment, confusion, condemnation, or simply avoidance. When they looked for assistance from their church on what the Bible says about the subject of divorce, they may be given a couple of Bible verses that do not seem apply to their individual circumstances. As a result, many divorcees eventually give up on God, the Bible, and the church.

If any of this describes your life, you have come to the right place – this book may be exactly what you have been searching for!

The author of this book – G.R. Holton – is a man that I value and treasure deeply. I first had the opportunity to meet G.R. back in 1981. Since that time, he has served as a mentor to me as I have served as a minister as well as a licensed marriage & family therapist.

The author has served as a minister for churches, the president of a children's home, an elder for his church, a licensed marriage & family therapist, and an author. G.R. is someone that I truly look up to, admire, and consider him a "father in the faith" as a fellow Christian.

One of the things that I have learned about G.R. is that he is an avid student of the Bible. In his church and professional work he has been deeply involved in assisting those who were dealing with divorce. I think that you will find that he is able to look at this subject both as a biblical scholar as well as a family therapist.

The author has really done a masterful job of looking at the "spirit" and the "truth" of this subject. He has tried to "go down the middle of the fairway" without veering to the left or the right.

G.R. has a heart for those who wrestle with the subject of divorce. He has the experience as a counselor in dealing with the tragedy of divorce. One of the things that many will probably find refreshing is that in this book he does not tell people what to do. Instead, he focuses on presenting the facts of what the Bible says, and then encourages individuals to make their own decisions.

In this book, the author is uniquely qualified to present this material from the perspective of both a minister and a marriage therapist. It is a true honor to be able to write the Foreword for this book. I encourage you to enjoy the fruit of his labor by reading this timely book!

John Klimko, Jr.
Licensed Marriage & Family Therapist

INTRODUCTION

This is a book is about biblical marriage for those who are divorced or remarried. However, those of you who are single, *again* due to the death of your mate may benefit from the interactive search on the subject. Marriage that conforms to God's Word is the happiest and most beautiful human relationship on earth. I know this from my own marriage of more than six decades! Although my marriage has stood the test of time there are many people, some very near and dear to me, have not been so fortunate. My purpose in writing this book is to help those of you who are divorced (single, *again*) or remarried find encouragement and hope from God's Word.

You probably never thought that your first marriage would end in divorce. In fact, the title of this book with "*again*" in italics followed by an exclamation point (!) indicates that you never expected to be single, *again!* According to statistics, being single *again*, depending on your age, is probably only a brief pause between one marriage and another. Now is a perfect time to focus on the basics of marriage as God defines it in the Bible.

I do not have all the answers about marriage in every situation. In fact, the principal theme of the book is that each person must find the answers for him or herself. I have seen just about every variation and circumstance of marriage and divorce in my thirty-plus years as a marital and family therapist, but I know other marital circumstances are out there. For example, we just started talking about internet adultery a few years ago! Some questions in some marriages beg for answers that I just do not know. This I do know: God will bless any sincere seeker for the truth with love and forgiveness.

This book will help you in your search, but you will need to do considerable work on your own. Read the Bible passages *as you read* through the book. Reading this book is an interactive experience. After all, isn't what the Bible teaches about marriage the only information that really matters? Commentaries and opinions, whether scholarly or conventional, are just that…commentaries and opinions!

This is not a theological treatise to advocate some doctrinal position on Biblical marriage, divorce and remarriage. Only the sincere individuals involved in the marriage/divorce/remarriage situation can know the *real* details of the matter and only they are responsible for their decisions.. This approach will not please everyone.

The individuals I want to reach with this message are those who *are* single, *again*. My approach is more therapeutic than theological. I use an interactive teaching format and try to avoid academic jargon. The message is: *Living single (again) following a divorce or death is both a great opportunity and a grave danger. You have a rare opportunity to really understand what God intended in biblical marriage, but at the same time you are a "street-wise" person threatened by both your past and future decisions. Your focus, whether unmarried or remarried, must be to please God.*

When a marriage ends either by divorce or death, the topic of biblical marriage becomes very relevant. What follows is a template for you to find answers to your questions from God's Word concerning biblical marriage following the end of your first marriage. I do not intend to debate anyone on the various important facets of this topic. I will *defend* any individual's right to search God's Word in making personal decisions on this very personal matter.

Marriage, divorce and remarriage are very important theological studies. Biblical scholars, and other sincere students of the Word, have provided numerous essays on the subject. I reference various wisdoms, beliefs, positions and commentaries sincere seekers may examine for themselves. See the section on the "Resources for Further Study" in the back of the book.

Marriage is an institution of God. It is natural for a man and woman to come together in marriage. We are created male and female by our Maker. Bible-believers go to the Scriptures for guidance, advice and affirmation on marriage. The primary focus of this book is to meet the needs of those who are single, *again* in adjusting to the changes in their lives in a way that maintains their faithfulness to God. A secondary purpose is to reduce the divorce rate among Christians, not add to it. As a happily married man for decades I have no real experience being single, *again*. But, as a family therapist, a minister and one whose family has experienced the horrors of divorce, the topic is very close to my heart.

Those in troubled marriages contemplating divorce should seek out qualified Christian marriage and family therapists *and* loving ministers of the gospel of Christ to "talk the walk" with them through this valley of death! The rest of us should study the topic with a heart of faith in God and a spirit of compassion toward anyone struggling with these issues. Nothing we can say or do will make any marriage "right" or "wrong" in God's eyes. Only the Lord can decide that! Nonetheless, we want every single, *again* Christian to have hope and to become stronger in the Lord. This guidebook is a statement of faith in your ability to do the right thing.

-Gresham R. Holton

Acknowledgments

This book has taken more than forty years to write! I could not name everyone who has contributed to this final outcome. The list would include many ministers and the members of several classes where it has been the subject of discussions. But I must name a few.

My Wednesday night adult class at Central Avenue in Valdosta has graciously collaborated with me through the materials three times over the past thirty years. Members of this class have asked good questions, as well as providing sound advice and personal commentary.

John Klimko, one of my ministers for the past thirty years and a respected marital and family therapist, has helped me make it therapeutic, rather than just another theological treatise.

Dr. Byron Brown, an erudite English professor, my good friend and fellow church leader, has contributed to both the content and the style. Byron has the unique ability of clear expression and vivid perception.

Myra Anderson, a retired research project manager and technical editor at Idaho National Laboratory and one of the most knowledgeable Bible scholars I know, has tirelessly read, revised, edited and improved the content. Myra continually reminded me of my chosen audience and helped me keep it personal.

I also acknowledge the contributions made by my friends and family for showing me both what biblical marriage is all about, but also about how lonely and painful it is to be single, *again*!

Gresham R. Holton

Chapter 1

Single, *Again*!

"WHERE DO I GO FROM HERE?"

Seeker's Task #1: *Prepare* to be a Super-Saint!

> *Your first task as a sincere seeker after God's will is to prepare to be and to live genuinely as a Christian! Study His Word for guidance. Trust your faith in Him. Live an example for others to follow. Become the best disciple of Christ you can be. Prepare to be a super-saint!*

"Divorce granted." You may have recently walked out of a courtroom after hearing these words. These words certified that a marriage was *legally* over. You may have been married for a few years, or much longer. The results are the same: your marriage has ended! These words also certified that you, your former mate or both of you, violated the vows you took

1

"till death do us part." Yet, you really_ *intended* for your marriage to last a lifetime!

You have now embarked on a new journey. It is journey typically traveled with pain, regrets, malice, unresolved conflicts, and lingering hurts. Forgiveness for yourself and for others seems so far away! You are probably confused and angry. The familiar networks of support such as church, family and friends seem to have crumbled in the emotional process of divorcing. You might think "Everyone hates me." You search for comfort and support from your spiritual roots, but even God seems far away! You desperately search for a "rule" or "prayer" or "spiritual reading" that assures that it is going to be alright. But it has become harder and harder to *even know* what is right.

Losing a mate in divorce is bad. *Really* bad! It affects so many people and changes so many lives! It might be one option to a bad marriage, but it is absolutely the worst option in the majority of cases. But the words "Divorce granted!" were spoken. The marriage *has* ended. Now what!? If you think getting a divorce ends your anxieties and troubles…think again!

LEARNING TO LIVE SINGLE

There are more single-again individuals in our world than ever before! Divorce is becoming more and more common. In fact, the world in which we live is challenging the very foundations of the institution of marriage. Just being married today is not what it was in the past century. In "Sociology 101" college freshmen are taught the *many* options for "doing marriage". For the first time in our history we are forced to *define* what we mean by "marriage". The traditional family of "Mom, Dad, and the kids" no longer defines the predominant American family! The fastest growing typical family in America today is the single-parent family. Many couples choose to cohabitate rather than legally marry. Our society has increasingly become worldly, with world-views that openly reject the traditional Judeo-Christian plan for marriage as defined in the Bible.

Finding the support you need at this time is not only difficult but outright dangerous for your spiritual welfare! You are looking for answers from the experts in our world, but ultimately you know you must seek out and discover the answers for yourself. That's a daunting task! If you are like most single-again Christians, you are desperately looking for help!

Spiritual Guides

First, you will probably seek help from your spiritual network. Churches in America and their literary advocates have long considered the topic of marriage to be a crucial study for spiritual doctrinal teaching. A casual walk through any Christian bookstore reveals a large section of books devoted to marriage, divorce and remarriage. A cursory inquiry for "God's Plan for Marriage" on the world-wide web will produce more than 2.6 million "hits"!

Marriage issues are hot topics in every church in America. All too often, a person's marital status seems to be more important to church membership than his or her personal faith in Christ! Whether or not you have ever been divorced is sometimes a litmus test for membership. Many times individuals who are divorced are made to feel like second-class citizens or even denied membership altogether!

The articles, books, and debates on doctrinal issues surrounding marriage and divorce and remarriage are numerous. Technical analysis of the original languages and Biblical interpretations abound to clarify the teachings on this subject[1], but most of us are not language scholars! Also, there is considerable disagreement among the scholars on marriage, divorce and remarriage from a biblical perspective.[2] We even disagree on the details of "how to *define* biblical marriage!"

Every church has been affected by this cultural shift in our society. Several churches are re-writing their covenants to more clearly define their tenets for marriage or to defend against internal conflicts over the question. Numerous churches, particularly the evangelical and other conservative churches, are openly disturbed as they try to deal with the question of biblical marriage. Fundamental membership questions about acceptable grounds for divorce and remarriage have been debated in these churches for years with a broad variety of results.

Sadly, fallout from these doctrinal debates has not made it easier for single, *again* Christians to do it right in marriage. The actual break-up of marriages by divorce, desertion or annulments continues to be high. Sometimes, after confronting the maze of doctrinal-correctness imbedded in a divorce and the feelings of rejection that follow; people simply abandon their faith! Others limp along accepting roles as "suspect members". Regardless, the marriage, divorce, remarriage trap has locked many into a life that is often more unhappy than happy, even if they try to remain church-connected and spiritually active. Divorced Christians too often look in vain for clear answers and social support from their church families! The fact is, rather than providing needed help, their church has often *added to the problems* for those caught up in this single, *again* maze! In many churches these saints might as well have a scarlet "A" painted on their foreheads. Divorcees and church membership does not seem to work. So, many confused and disheartened saints just drop out! This is a time when you really need your spiritual foundations for future building.

Single, Again! Because of Death

Another group of single, *again* Christians are those who have lost their mates to death. Bill had just lost his wife of more than thirty-three years to cancer. "My world is just *empty!*" he lamented as he tried to assess his situation in life. He and Jody had worked as a minister-wife team to provide spiritual strength for others. Now he felt very alone. Bob, who also was widowed because of cancer, said he just felt "out of place". He said, "It was always Bob and Virginia, and now it is just Bob!" Just a casual dinner with friends was difficult for Bob without Virginia to help carry the conversation. Like many others, these two men became single, *again* because of death! Although single, *again* divorcees are the primary focus of this study, Christian widows and widowers face many of the same issues.

These Christians know the pain of being single, *again* after a marriage that was "made in heaven"! Where *do you go* from here? Whether by an act of God (death) or an act of man (divorce) being a "single, *again*" Christian is a challenge! The loneliness is deadening, but other issues such as forgiveness (or not), coping with guilt, maintaining Christian purity, and rebuilding trust and hope are often daily threats to spiritual health! Being single after the security of marriage is *scary* …and very dangerous!

Even though cultural pressure has changed how we define the institution of marriage, it is still the norm in America. In fact, if a person remains single beyond an "older than young" age, others start attempting to be matchmakers! Regardless, 46% of the population 25 years old and older was single in the 2000 census. In both the Old and New Testaments, marriage was the norm, but *remaining single* was also practiced. Our world has viewed "living single" in many different ways. Living single is not the norm, nor is it a simple easy life for a Christian.

Statistics show that you will more than likely decide to remarry within five years of your divorce. We understand that you do not intend to be a celibate. You might ask therefore, "why are we even talking about being single if remarriage is a probability?" One major reason is that you need to understand the importance of sexual involvement and your spiritual health. Both secular history and the Bible contrast your spiritual health and sexual activities. As noted above, depending on your age, one of the dangers you now face is maintaining sexual purity. In both history and the Bible, spiritual celibacy is the highest form of spiritual sexual commitment. Although you probably do not intend to make such a spiritual commitment, that is exactly what you must do regarding sexual activities while you are unmarred.

History and "Living Single"

The world of the Greeks and Romans sometimes encouraged marriage, but sex apart from marriage was acceptable. Some Greek philosophers thought marriage was an encumbrance on sexual activity. When Diogenes was asked about the right time to marry, he replied: *For a young man not yet; for an old man never at all.*

A form of celibacy was commonly practiced by the priests of Greek Cybelle and the Roman Vestal Virgins, but marriage was still the norm for both Greeks and Romans. In fact, the Roman aristocracy, due to declining birth rates, urged marriage and children. Plutarch called marriage a "sacred sowing". According to him citizens should not marry unless they were willing to produce offspring. Bearing children was also the practical function of marriage in most of the ancient world.

According to the writings of Josephus and the Dead Sea scrolls, the Jewish sect known as the Essenes generally practiced celibacy. However, the Dead Sea scrolls revealed that they also practiced marriage and divorce. Certain of their number who were especially pious abstained from all sexual activity and marriage. Traditions from much earlier give examples of others who lived single due to religious devotion or necessity. Celibacy was also an Old Testament practice.[3]

The Bible and "Living Single"

Contrasting the differences in the life of a single (unmarried) person and a married person from the perspective of the Bible will also be helpful. First, we must understand our natures, or how God made us in the beginning. The Bible describes how the first single, Adam, was later given a wife, Eve!: *"So God created man in His own image; in the image of God He created him; male and female He created them."* (Genesis 1:27) The key words are "male" and "female" . . . created by God! Then, he sanctioned these two with a blessing: *"Be fruitful and multiply; fill the earth and subdue it".* To no one's surprise, men and women are different! Two facts: 1). Two singles, different genders as "male" and "female"; 2) The conception and birth of children was the natural result of the "two becoming one"! Sexual activities are clearly implied in this passage.

For Bible-believing Christians, *sexual relations define a major difference in "living single" and living "married":* Men and women use their God-given "maleness" and "femaleness" as one way of relating to each other! A review of the Bible texts on sexual immorality illustrates how marriage sanctifies the sexual interactions of "males" with "females". In the very beginning of time, Adam and Eve *"knew each other"* and were not ashamed. (Genesis 2:24-25). In the first Biblical marriage, sexual relations had the approval of the Creator and resulted in replenishing the earth with offspring.

However, very strict laws of God forbade sexual relations outside of marriage (Deuteronomy 22:13-30), and violations of these laws could result in death (Leviticus 20:10-20). Christians are warned to not even *"keep company"* with a sexually immoral person (I Corinthians 5:1-13).   In this example, Paul condemned "a brother" (fellow-Christian) who <u>had</u> (was sexually involved with) his "father's wife".

In the Bible, living single clearly implies celibacy, or abstaining from sexual relations. Thus, any consideration about living single must include a study on the Biblical doctrine of "celibacy". The Apostle Paul (See 1 Corinthians 7:1-2) defined celibacy with a single statement: *"It is good for a man not to touch a woman".* However, the following verse honors the institution of marriage: *"Nevertheless, because of sexual immorality let each man have his own wife, and let each wife have her own husband." (vs. 2)*

Yet, notable biblical singles include John the Baptist, Jesus, and the Apostle Paul. Christians certainly may remain single rather than marry. It is biblically-okay to live your life as a single person following the end of your marriage.

However, if you seek to be right with God, you must maintain sexual purity. Sexual activities are sanctioned by God *only in the institution of marriage*!   Any sexual activity outside of marriage according to the Bible, is sexual immorality: *"Marriage is honorable in all, and the **bed undefiled**: but whoremongers and adulterers God will judge."* (Hebrews 13:4).

Choosing to Live Single

What does the Bible say about living single? In a word, if you decide to live single and not marry, your first task is to assess your present situation and *prepare* to be a super-saint! Not only does this define commitment to God that will be required of you, but it is a way to remind you of the wonderful opportunity you have to serve God.

It will be useful to review a few biblical references that summarize, or express composite truths for *any individual's* piety with God. Our list will be general, and not exhaustive. The search should epitomize the question: *"What does any individual look like who is striving to be right with God?* What should be his or her world views, or character values, or personal goals for life? In short, we will attempt to describe the principles and standards for the ideal Christian individual!

BIBLICAL "SUPER SAINTS"

All of us want to be the perfect devout ideal Christian. Setting our standards as *the ideal* is a worthy goal. Jesus *did* say, *"Be ye perfect"*(Matthew 5:48). But, we are the first to admit that no one of us *is* perfect. We are all imperfect individuals who often fail. We married flawed individuals whose sins probably became more obvious in marriage than before marriage. Nonetheless, we continue to hold high the *ideal* (as we should) for what God expects. How do we do this with an individual Christian? What would that person look like? How would you describe his or her lifestyle?

Read: Mark 10:17-22

A wealthy young man came to Jesus with a question: *"Good Teacher, what shall I do to inherit eternal life"?* First, he was told to keep the Ten Commandments. To this the man replied, *"This I have done from my youth up!"* Then Jesus said, *"Go, sell all that you have and give it to the poor".* This young man must have thought he was so close to "perfection" that he wanted to know the one or two things he had missed! This story of a proud young aristocrat reveals that God never expected to find us perfect or ideal! However, any true seeker must start with just one goal*: to please God!* This then translates into two imperatives: *"Know the will of God"* and *"Do it!"* That is neither simple nor easy! However, there are some principles that guide us to build a framework for defining the

9

"ideal" Christian…one who knows what pleases God, and does it!

A careful reading of Jesus' sermon-on-the-mount (Matthew 5-7) and other scriptures that describe God's expectations for us will help us outline a composite picture of *the ideal*. The list that follows is long, but far from exhaustive! You could add many other passages, but…hey! *You actually should include the entire Bible!* The point is that we are at the best *imperfect* people who strive *to be perfect*. Use the short list of principles below to suggest an outline picture of the perfect Christian:

IS COMMITTED TO GOD - *Matthew 6:33: "But seek first the kingdom of God and His righteousness, an all these things shall be added to you."*

DOES THE RIGHT THING - *Matthew 5:20: "For I say to you, that unless your righteousness exceeds the righteousness of the scribes and Pharisees, you will by no means enter the kingdom of heaven."*

HAS A RIGHT HEART - *Matthew 5:20: "For I say to you, that unless your righteousness exceeds the righteousness of the scribes and Pharisees, you will by no means enter the kingdom of heaven."*

TRUSTS IN GOD - *Matthew 7:7: "Ask, and it will be given to you; seek, and you will find; knock, and it will be opened to you. For everyone who asks receives, and he who seeks finds, and to him who knocks it will be opened."*

DOES NOT JUDGE OTHERS - *Matthew 7:1: "Judge not, that you be not judged. For with what judgment you judge, you will be judged; and with the same measure you use, it will be measured back to you."*

LOVES GOD AND OTHERS - *Matthew 22:37: "'You shall love the Lord your God with all your heart, with all your soul, and with all your mind.' This is the first and great commandment. And the second is like it: 'You shall love your neighbor as yourself'"*

IS FORGIVEN AND FORGIVES - *Matthew 6:14 "For if you forgive men their trespasses, you heavenly father will also forgive you. But if you do not forgive men their trespasses, neither will your Father forgive your trespasses."*

LIVES BY THE GOLDEN RULE *(Matthew 7:12), Luke 6:31) ETC...ETC...ETC...*

One question: Would everyone who is an ideal Christian, please stand up? *"None is righteous, no not one!"* But that does not excuse any of us to ignore our sins and weaknesses. This list should motivate us to be the best we can be! The first step in moving on is *to reaffirm the ideal standard for living as a single Christian!* Resolve to be the best that you can be, whether you are unmarried or married.

Singles in the Bible

In the New Testament marriage was the norm; but *remaining single* was also an option. *"Forbidding to marry"*, or the doctrine of *enforced celibacy*, was defined as a doctrine of demons. (I Timothy 4:1-4). Jesus helps us organize our thoughts about being married or unmarried in His response to questions from the Pharisees as they *tested* him.

Read: Matthew 19:3-12

In this passage Jesus reaffirmed marriage as originally instituted by God in the beginning (Genesis chapters 1-2). God made them "male and female" implying the sexual content of this relationship. His point is that *from the beginning* sexual activities were always restricted to the marital relationship. Thus, confirming that any sexual activity outside of marriage is immoral and constitutes grounds for breaking up a marriage!

> *His disciples said to Him, "If such is the case of the man with his wife, it is better not to marry." 11* But He said to them, "All cannot accept this saying, but only those to whom it has been given: *12* For there are eunuchs who were born thus from their mother's womb, and there are eunuchs who were made eunuchs by men, and there are eunuchs who have made themselves eunuchs for the kingdom of heaven's sake. He who is able to accept it, let him accept it.

These listeners opted for being unmarried rather than marriage *if sexual activities were restricted to marriage* and the *probable* violations thereof! To them living single appeared to be the best way to live. (See Chapter 7 for more details on this passage).

Living single in the Bible implied living *a celibate life!* It is very difficult for a normal man or a normal woman to refrain from sexual activities. Sexual needs are natural emotional drives for both men and women. God created us with these urges, "male and female" (Genesis 1:27). Jesus concluded this discussion by saying *"He who is able to accept it, let him accept it"* (Matthew 19:12). The point is that most men and women will feel compelled to satisfy their sexual needs and thus *could not live* a celibate life.

In the First Corinthian letter Paul defines sexual immorality as a unique and highly destructive sin. First, Paul rebukes them for their attitude toward an incestuous relationship (1 Corinthians 5:1-8). Then, he directly tells them not even to keep company with a sexually immoral brother (5:9-12). Finally after a brief interlude on legal matters he warned them against the uniquely destructive nature of sexual immorality. (6:12-20).

This has been a rather extended analysis of what living single meant in the Bible. My purpose for such a review is to help you understand what will be involved for you if you choose this lifestyle. God created you "male" or "female" with powerful urges for sexual union. The force of these created hormones may vary in individuals according to age and experience, but nonetheless, deciding to live single will be a challenging choice.

THREAT OF SEXUAL IMMORALITY

Sexual immorality is a unique sin, not because it is more condemned than others, but because it attacks so much of what is the core of our service to God and our self-respect. Understanding why it is unique forms a foundation for future considerations about marriage and divorce.

In an odd way, sexual activity has often been associated with extreme spirituality. There were temple prostitutes in New Testament days. In fact, one of the common characteristics of many cults is the form of *sexual morality* or *immorality* practiced. For some, it was the *denial* of any sexual pleasures, while for others it was the *indulgence* in all sorts of sexual encounters. For example David Koresh and the Branch Davidians were known to have practiced very bizarre sexual behaviors. But, on the other hand, the rise of ascetic orders such as the Benedictines confirmed man's quest to be right with God by refraining from any sexual activities! Sexual involvement, or the abstinence from it, was in both cases an attempt to emulate the ideal state of being a Christian, -- to become a "super-saint"!

So, it should not surprise us to know that many who wanted to do it right with God in the past chose refraining from sexual activities as an important plank in their platforms! Paul identified the historical past for some in the Corinthian church.

Read 1st Corinthians 6:9-11

Do you not know that the unrighteous will not inherit the kingdom of God? Do not be deceived. Neither fornicators, nor idolaters, nor adulterers, nor homosexuals, nor sodomites, nor thieves, nor covetous, nor drunkards, nor revilers, nor extortioners will inherit the kingdom of God. And such were some of you. But you were washed, but you were sanctified, but you were justified in the name of the Lord Jesus and by the Spirit of our God.

Compulsive Sexual Activities

Then Paul explains the importance of this subject by showing how addictive sexual activities can become. Habits may be defined as repeated behaviors. In fact, a repeated behavior that becomes a *compulsive* habit is clinically defined as an *"addiction"*! The personal loss of control in an addiction is the first sign of degradation in sexual immorality. If left uncontrolled, sexual activities can become devastating to the faith of a saint. So, even if it is legal or acceptable socially, it may become a therapeutic addiction. The Apostle Paul noted this problem when he said, *All things are lawful for me, but all things are not helpful. All things are lawful for me, but I will not be brought under the power (*addiction*) of any.*(1 Corinthians 6:12)

A Sin against God

The Apostle finally makes a clear statement of the fact that God is interested in our bodies for the resurrection (1 Corinthians 6:13-14). Paul waits until later (1 Corinthians 15) to defend the doctrine of the resurrection, but for the moment he declares it as the basis for sexual *morality* in this life. They were living in a way that degrades the body's worth in the eyes of God. In Paul's words, the **"body is not for immorality"**; the body is **"for the Lord,"** and **"the Lord is for the body."** God did not create the body with its sexual capabilities and drives to satisfy these desires indiscriminately. God made man's physical body for *His purposes*, ultimately to bring glory to Himself.

Paul's conclusion is clear in verse 20: *"**Therefore glorify God in your body.**"* We are not to use our bodies to serve ourselves, but to serve God. This concept was directly opposed to both the libertine practices of the Corinthians and the ascetic approach of the Gnostics. The Gnostics tried to separate the matters of the worldly "body" and the spiritual "spirit". Paul confirmed the holistic nature of the body and spirit, saying that *"the Lord is for the body."*

False teachers tend to cater to the desires of the flesh, while Jesus and His apostles call upon us to take up our crosses and to crucify the flesh and its desires:

Read Romans 6:12-13

Therefore do not let sin reign in your mortal body that you should obey its lusts, and do not go on presenting the members of your body to sin as <u>instruments of unrighteousness</u>; but present yourselves to God as those alive from the dead, and your members as <u>instruments of righteousness</u> to God.

Read Romans 8:12-13

So then, brethren, we are under obligation, not to the flesh, to live according to the flesh— for if you are living according to the flesh, you must die; but if by the Spirit you are putting to death the deeds of the body, you will live .

15

Therefore consider the members of your earthly body as dead to immorality, impurity, passion, evil desire, and greed, which amounts to idolatry (Colossians 3:5).

So, it should not surprise us to know that many in the past who wanted to do it right with God chose refraining from sexual activities or indulging in sexual activities as marks of being a "super saint".

Read 1st Corinthians 6:16-20

Do you not know that the unrighteous will not inherit the kingdom of God? Do not be deceived. Neither fornicators, nor idolaters, nor adulterers, nor homosexuals, nor sodomites, nor thieves, no covetous, nor drunkards, nor revilers, nor extortionists will inherit the kingdom of God. And such were some of you. But you were washed, but you were sanctified, but you were justified in the name of the Lord Jesus and by the Spirit of our God.

A Spiritual Sin

We often debate whether or not one sin is worse than another. No one denies that some sins will have more dire consequences for us and perhaps for other people (our mates, families) than some other sins. We also know that sin is a violation of God's law that literally attacks the fiber of our spirituality. Sexual immorality is an offense against God, *(*Romans 11:36*)* but it is also a sin against our Lord Jesus Christ. It is a frontal attack upon the very temple of the Holy Spirit. This makes sexual immorality a unique sin!

Note these words of the Bible:

Do you not know that your bodies are members of Christ? Shall I then take away the members of Christ and make them members of a harlot? May it never be! Or do you not know that the one who joins himself to a harlot is one body with her? For He says, "The two will become one flesh." But the one who joins himself to the Lord is one spirit with Him. (1 Corinthians 6:15-17)

In the context of this passage, Paul insists that one cannot be one in spirit with the Savior and one in the flesh with a harlot. What is done spiritually does directly relate to what is done in the body. We cannot separate our bodies (activities) from our spirituality! He concludes this passage defining the unique destructiveness of sexual immorality with:

Flee sexual immorality. Every sin that a man does is outside the body, but he who commits sexual immorality sins against his own body. <u>*Or do you not know that your body is the temple of the Holy Spirit who is in you, whom you have from God, and you are not your own?*</u> *For you were bought at a price; therefore glorify God in your body and in your spirit, which are God's.* (1 Corinthians 6:18-20)

Therefore, the overarching principle that governs sexual activities for anyone that is single (or, for that matter, anyone else) is this: *"therefore glorify God in (y)our body"* (verse 20).

In summary, practicing celibacy (abstaining from sexual relations) is one way Christians have attempted to be super saints, abstaining completely from sexual relations for short periods of time or for a lifetime! The purpose of the denial of sexual relations and the goal in both cases is *to live faithful lives for the Lord.* This goal is the driving force that motivated these saints to be as good as they could be! They were striving after the elusive goal: *being the ideal Christian!*

Dangers facing Single, *Again* Christians

So, as a single, *again* Christian, the pressures of sexual needs could result in the unique sin of sexual immorality. This is why Paul said *young widows* should marry, while instructing the church to support *older widows*. (I Timothy 5:4-14). In a different case, Paul gave different instructions to *a married couple* (1 Corinthians 7:5) and *young virgins* (1 Corinthians 7:36). He also tempered all these instructions (See 1 Corinthians 7) with *a person's current life situations*, stating that because of the present distress (7:26) each individual may have different options.

On the other hand, Paul makes a strong argument against permanent departing (divorcing) to break up a marriage, even if it is a marriage between a believer and an unbeliever (1 Corinthians 7:10-16). The basic principle is clear: *biblical marriage is preferred over living as a single.*

In conclusion, your biblical roadmap for completing *Task #1* after you became "single, *again*" is clearly outlined in the following passage:

> *If then you have been raised up with Christ, <u>keep seeking the things above</u>, where Christ is, seated at the right hand of God. 2 <u>Set your mind on the things above</u>, not on the things that are on earth. For you have died and <u>your life is hidden with Christ in God</u>. When Christ, who is our life, is revealed, then you also will be revealed with Him in glory. Therefore <u>consider the members of your earthly body as dead to immorality</u>, impurity, passion, evil desire, and greed, which amounts to idolatry. For it is on account of these things that the wrath of God will come, and in them you also once walked, when you were living in them.* (Colossians 3:1-7)

We will keep bringing you back to this thought: *Just be a strong, faithful, pure Christian whether you are* single, *again* or remarried*!*

Chapter 2

Marriage:

SEEKING THE *IDEAL* MARRIAGE

Seeker's Task #2: <u>*Learn*</u> from the Loss of Your Marriage

You are now single, again! Your previous life of being married may be over, but this is a good time for you to re-examine what the term "biblical marriage" is all about. You can learn from your loss. Go back to the beginning when you first said "I do". Your task for this chapter is to re-connect with your understanding of the ideal biblical marriage.

Single, *AGAIN*?! WOW! Several words could be used to describe this new, unfamiliar marital state that follows the loss of your marriage. Dazed! Rejected! Abandoned! Empty! Shocked! Alone! Your life has slowly (yet *suddenly*!) gone from being scheduled and well-organized to one of chaos, indecision and *lost*-ness! "Divorce is not (just) an event. It is a process. You grow through that process a minute, an hour, a day, a week at a time."[1] The loss following the death of a mate is no less life-changing: This also is a good time for you to re-connect your understanding of marriage to biblical marriage. One person said it like this: 'Coming home to an empty house is not easy. There is no one to greet you, and the chair opposite yours at the dinner table is empty. The house seems to echo from the silence and you shed a tear as you remember that you are now alone. So many years together, so many memories you two created together are all you have left. Losing a loved one changes your entire life, especially when the loved one was also your best friend"[5].

What has happened?! How has this happened to me? When your marriage journey started you intended for it to last forever! *Right?!* Now it may seem like you are in a wild nightmare, looking back over a terrible wreck. Experiencing the pain and anguish of it all and wishing you could wake up! You look back over your marriage and try to *remember…*maybe it was just a bad marriage, or maybe a good-marriage-gone bad! If it was a good marriage, why did it have to end!? A marriage that ended by death often leaves the surviving mate with the same confusing feelings. The more you try to make sense out of it, the more confusing it can become. The information that follows may or may not be your understanding of what defines marriage. We want to review it to form a baseline of basics for those of you seeking biblical marriage.

DEFINING THE IDEAL MARRIAGE

Marriage is one of two states that are possible: married (with a mate) or *not* married (single). That's simple, but true! You are either *married* or *single* (not married). The *legal* lines that separate these categories are very sharp and distinct, but the *emotional* boundaries separating them are painted with broad grey strokes! Our greatest spiritual and emotional dangers concerning marriage are in those grey emotional boundaries just *before* the marriage began and *just after* the marriage ended. Therefore due to these dangers, it is useful to re-examine our own ideas compared with God's standards regarding Biblical marriage.

What is marriage, anyway? There are as many answers to this question as there are cultures, religions, and histories in the world! Marriage was defined as simply "jumping over a broom" by the slaves in southern United States in pre-Civil War days. In West Africa those who crossed the boundary from being single to married had to go through elaborate blood-letting ceremonies. The institution of marriage was here before any other human institution existed! Marriage has been defined in various ways in every age and culture.

J. D. Thomas says: *"...a marriage exists when an eligible man and woman 'decide that they are married'".*[6] This definition, he argues, can be used to define the first marriages recorded in the Bible as well as the marriage of a marooned couple on a desert island. This definition might include the modern practice of "living-together" co-habitation as one form of common law marriage. Showers has stated that marriage is: *"God's act of joining a man and a woman in a permanent, covenanted, one-flesh relationship*" [7] This definition places more emphasis on marriage as an act of God designed to be permanent. Here the emphasis is more on the mutual commitments in a marriage, rather than just social co-habitation.

Biblical Marriage

What is *"biblical marriage"*? You may think this question is too technical since this book is for those who are single, *again*. It is not our intention to provide either technical, theological or legal arguments to define the boundaries of marriage. But you do need to reaffirm your understanding of the basics of marriage so that you can *decide for yourself!* Several important questions can help you see the difference in being married or single. These are inquiries you should make at this time. How does it help to *know* what went wrong? What can you *learn from this terrible experience* that will help you *grow closer to God*?

First, understand that we are talking about "ideal" as the *perfect standard* to which everyone aspires. Yes, that's a lofty definition for biblical marriage! Another way to define "ideal biblical marriage" is to describe it as it was before sin entered the world. Go back to *the beginning* with Adam and Eve for a refresher course on *how* marriage was intended to work as established by God. This information gives us the model by which all other marriages should be evaluated, including your previous marriage and any future marriage. Few marriages actually become the *ideal* biblical marriage, but the *ideal* model must be the baseline! So, what can you learn by re-examining the first marriage?

Relationship of Man and Woman

First, we need to review "*who*" was married. Adam, the first *man* was married by God to Eve, the first *woman*. Biblical marriage is a union of a man and a woman. Basic!

READ Matthew 19:1-6

> *And He answered and said to them, "Have you not read that He who made them at the beginning 'made them male and female,'* 5 and said, 'For this reason a man shall (1) <u>leave his father and mother</u> and (2) <u>be joined to his wife</u>, and the two shall (3) <u>become one flesh</u>'? 6 So then, they are no longer two but one flesh. (Matthew 19:4-6)

Marriage *in the beginning* was a matter of "*leaving*" and "*cleaving*" It involved a male and female "*parting*" from their families of origin and "*joining*" each other. It was further defined by the phrase, "*they shall become one flesh*"- a reference to both sexual intercourse and forming a single legal entity which might include the bearing of children.

These verses outline three essential characteristics that serve as guidelines to define the boundaries of biblical marriage.

First, marriage in the Bible was *a public act* of leaving a family of origin, one's parents, to begin a new family. The Hebrew word for "leave" means to "leave behind" or "depart from", or to "let go". The "leaving" happened when God took the rib from *man* and made a *woman* to be the mate (helpmeet), whom He brought to the man to be his wife (Genesis 2:22). Thus the Bible reveals that in the first marriage two people were joined together and publicly set forth as husband and wife . The key word is *"public"* presentation of Adam and Eve as joined. In addition, the "joining together" of Adam and Eve resulted in the bearing of children .

Secondly, the two people enter into *a permanent bond* with each other. The husband now will *cleave to* (be joined to) his wife" and the wife will *cleave to* (be joined to) her husband. This becomes a contract, or covenant. A covenant in Old Testament usage was a pact between two people who made a commitment of loyalty and faithfulness. A covenant usually contained *promises* (grants) and *vows* (including penalties) for compliance or non-compliance. The word *cleave* means to "cling", or "keep close" or, to "stick like glue". The word also carries the connotation of loyalty and affection. It described Ruth's affection for Naomi (Ruth 1:14) and how David's faithful soldiers stuck with him (2 Samuel 20:2). Like the love of Jesus (*agape* –sacrificial commitment), the love of a husband and wife binds them to each other like glue. Modern marriage promises and vows help define these marriage bonds.

Finally, the *male* and *female* who had made the permanent bond of commitment formed *a physical/social union* where the two "become one". This phrase refers to the physical sexual union of the male and female; however, it also underscores the holistic unity that marriage affects in basic companionship qualities such as shared time and common goals. In the words of the Bible, a married couple "become one" as their commitments, promises, and vows to each other are literally lived out in their lives! Procreation, bearing children, usually follows in this sacred environment. Bearing and rearing children for future generations was accomplished through this intimate relationship.

ROLES AND DUTIES IN THE MARRIAGE

A second consideration in understanding Biblical marriage is to see *how* it was put together. What were the roles of the males and the females, and the duties each had to each other and to God? A good understanding of the roles of husbands and wives will further help you define marriage. Many issues that destroy marriages arise from the differences in men and women and how they function in the marriage. Many of these marital functions are defined by the gender, male or female, of the husband and wife.

READ Genesis 2:15-25

In the beginning God put marriages together (Adam and Eve) with language that both defined marriage and instructed us on marital duties for the man and the woman. These insights are clustered around three over-arching principles in the opening chapters of the Bible (Genesis 1-3).

First, Man _and_ woman were created *in the image* of a loving, all-powerful, all-wise and eternal God to carry on His work on earth.

*Then God blessed _them_, and God said to _them_, Be fruitful and multiply; fill the earth and subdue it; have dominion over the fish of the sea, over the birds of the air, and over every living thing that moves on the earth." (*Genesis 1:28).

Notice how that "the image of God" was in both of them! Both were assigned authority over God's created world.

Second, *Unique roles and responsibilities* for men and women were to be _leadership_, dominance, for men and _helper_, submissiveness, for women.

> *And the Lord God caused a deep sleep to fall on Adam, and he slept; and He took one of his ribs, and closed up the flesh in its place. 22 Then the rib which the Lord God had taken from man He made into a woman, and He brought her to the man. 23 And Adam said: "This is now bone of my bones and flesh of my flesh; She shall be called Woman, because she was taken out of Man.* (Genesis 2:16-25)

Their unique roles were illustrated by the fact that Adam was created first, then Eve. The symbolic characteristic of Eve being taken from the rib of man implied the roles of authority and submission in their relationships to each other. (See also 1 Corinthians 11:8-10). The Apostle Paul's commentary on the unique relationship of leadership and submissiveness in marriage elevated the marital roles of husbands and wives by comparing them to Christ and His church. (Ephesians 5:22-24)

Third, Adam and Eve (both) were told to *"tend the garden"* and *"not eat of the tree of the knowledge of good and evil"*. (Genesis 2:16-20)

Thus created in the image of God, Adam and Eve were given specific role relationships and placed in positions as caretakers of God's creation. They were granted authority to care for the garden. They had the privilege to eat from *all the trees* but *one*, the tree of the knowledge of good and evil. At this point, the first married couple fell from the grace of God and corrupted God's world with sin.

> *So when the woman saw that the tree was good for food, that it was pleasant to the eyes, and a tree desirable to make one wise, she took of its fruit and ate. She also gave to her husband with her, and he ate. 7 Then the eyes of both of them were opened, and they knew that they were naked; and they sewed fig leaves together and made themselves coverings.* (Genesis 3:6-7)

So sin changed the "ideal" to the "real" world of today! The fall of man from the Garden of Eden because of sin brought terrible negative consequences for both man and woman for all creation including marriage. Then to Adam He said,

> *"Because you have heeded the voice of your wife, and have eaten from the tree of which I commanded you, saying, 'You shall not eat of it': Cursed is the ground for your sake; in toil you shall eat of it all the days of your life".* (Genesis 3:17)

It is significant to note that not only were the roles different for the male and the female, but the consequences of their sins were also different. The dire consequences from Eve's sin have been felt in the painful delivery of children ever since. On the other hand, Adam's task to *"subdue the earth"* did not change; but after the fall, *"thorns and thistles"* would forever challenge man and make his task much more difficult. The key word is "different", but punishing! Both Adam and Eve violated the trust placed in them by

God. They broke faith with Him. Both of them were punished, but their punishments were based on their gender.

A SACRED SEXUAL PARTNERSHIP

Your study of the beginning of marriage in the Bible (Genesis 1:26-2:25) has revealed that marriage originated when woman was formed literally out of man and they were joined together! Their task as the first married couple was to do the work of God in the Garden. The work of God was to faithfully obey Him in caring for and living in the Garden. They were to be a close knit team bearing the very image of God.

The actual creation of woman from the man's body typifies the intimate closeness between the male and female in marriage. It also pre-shadows why sexual immorality was defined as the ultimate violation of the marital compact. Biblical marriage was a sexual partnership based on a covenant of trust. This intimacy is clearly reflected in the words of Adam: *"This is now bone of my bones And flesh of my flesh; She shall be called Woman, Because she was taken out of Man."*

An old joke speaks of God coming to Adam to tell him that He wanted to make a perfect companion for him by creating woman. "She would be someone", God continued, "very much like him with similar wants and needs". This woman would be the perfect "helpmeet" for him to get his work done that had been assigned by God. She would be the perfect sexual counterpart for him. She would fulfill all his needs sexually, emotionally, and physically. Hearing how wonderful and perfect for man woman was going to be, Adam asked God what a woman like this would cost. "Oh," God responded, "A companion like that would be worth an "arm and a leg" to a man! To which Adam responded, "What can I get for a spare rib?"

Intimacy in marriage was described as *"bone of my bones"* and *"becoming one flesh"*. Two very gender-different partners (male and female) *become one flesh* through the process of both working together and living together, *intimately*! Each can almost get into the skin of the other! They were commissioned *together* with the task to rule over God's creation and to represent God in His creation. They had a joint duty to faithfully perform in both tasks. The *two* were to act as *one*. Nothing illustrated this better than sexual intercourse.

Marital closeness was further reflected in their commitment to each other; and it was protected by the promises and vows exchanged in a public way. Their intention to dwell together *exclusively with each other* to do God's work *together* was *publicly* announced to the whole world. Personal, *exclusive* intimacy as the wife of one man or husband of one woman was the baseline of faithfulness to this commitment. They were bound together in a unity of intimacy that could only be breached by the sin of sexual immorality. Under the Law of Moses this partnership was protected by the penalty of public disgrace and stoning to death of those who violated it. (Leviticus 20:10-20)

The Cycle of Independence and Dependence

The cycle of independence and dependence is continued by the procreation of children. The resulting offspring grow and develop in the knowledge of God (Deuteronomy 6) as they move toward independence from the parents. Then, at some point, the children leave the father and mother and cleave to their mate in marriage. At that point the cycle of dependence to independence starts all over again with a new husband-wife partnership to represent God and to bear children.

Several principles about marriage are evident from this life cycle description:

1) *The sexual relationship, and the procreation of children, was an important part of the marital relationship.*

   Although propagation is not the sole purpose of marriage, from an Old Testament point of view, it was very important. A childless wife was viewed negatively.

2) *Training a child in the way he should go was basic to Old Testament parenting.* (See Deuteronomy 6; Proverbs 22:6).

   In addition to the training to survive on the earth, a child was taught to reverence God and to respect the parents. The importance of this generation-bridging training is underscored by the fact that a child who did not learn to obey the parents would not live long on the earth (See Ephesians 6:1) Disobedience to parents could result in death for the child.

3) *Duties and responsibilities for training and protecting children and women were clustered around the parental roles of fathers and of husbands.*

This further supported the role relationships in the marriage. The male in the partnership had the basic duty of leadership in training and protecting the children. A woman's obedience was transferred from her father to her husband at marriage.

Organized with Role Responsibilities

In addition to the sexual partnership that produced children (conjugal rights), a marriage also included duties to provide food, clothing and shelter, or the physical survival necessities of life. These elements come under the function of toiling to survive after the fall. (See Genesis 3:17-20; Exodus 21:10-11). Fathers were responsible for provisions and protection for their wives and children. When a marriage occurred, the new husband was then responsible for the wife and for any subsequent children. The husband (or father) was required to be faithful to his wife and children so that they would physically survive. Before sin entered, God provided everything. After the fall, man was responsible to provide.

The cycle of *submission* of wives and children and *leadership* of husbands and fathers bridged the generations from the biological parental family to the marital family. This cycle was mirrored in the role-duties of husbands and wives. The male was to be the "leader" and the female was to be the "helpmeet".

The male was the leader of the marriage partnership by order of creation. (I Corinthians 11:1-6) The female was the "helpmeet" (suitable helper), who in submission helped accomplish the work of the marriage. Her signal function as child-bearer was perhaps the most powerful role for her current world and for future generations.

In summary, in the beginning the Old Testament definitions for marriage denoted a man (Adam) and a woman (Eve), both created in the image of God. The two were joined together (married) to represent God on earth and to rule or subdue God's creation according to his commands. As sexual partners they were to multiply (themselves) and replenish the earth (with children).

This beginning ideal model for Biblical marriage had these three general components:

1) A permanent _sexual partnership_ between one man and one woman,
2) The _marriage tasks_ were to do God's work of a): caring for (ruling) his creation and b): supplying future generations with children (men and women for marriage),
3) The institution was _protected by sexual exclusiveness_ for the marital partners. The penalty for violating this sexual exclusiveness was death.

The history of the Old Testament shows that this model was grossly corrupted. Kostenberger chronicles six violations of God's ideal marriage model that historically corrupted biblical marriage: polygamy, divorce, adultery, homosexuality, sterility, and the dilution of the gender distinctions between males and females.[8]

When Satan entered the picture the state of marriage was corrupted by sin and everything changed. The ideal world that was before the fall became what it is today, the real world of sinful imperfections! This corruption of the very state of marriage, with man in control rather than God, resulted in a history of abuses. Marital structure changed drastically from the ideal in the years that followed and even up to the time of Christ! That does not make it right, but it helps explain the difference between living in an ideal world and the real world.

Back to the Future

Several New Testament passages combine to further define the biblical model for marriage. These passages should be studied against the ideal model that was originated by God at the beginning.

The ideal marriage model of the Old Testament was referenced three times in the New Testament indicating that the basic plan for marriage was the same from the beginning through the days of the New Testament, notwithstanding the corrupting influence of sin.

> Matthew 19:5 *For this reason a man shall leave his father and mother and be joined to his wife, and the two shall become one flesh'*

> Mark 10:6-8 *But from the beginning of the creation, God 'made them male and female.' 7 'For this reason a man shall leave his father and mother and be joined to his wife, 8 and the two shall become one flesh'; so then they are no longer two, but one flesh.*

> Ephesians 5:31 *For this reason a man shall leave his father and mother and be joined to his wife, and the two shall become one flesh.*

While God's eternal plan is much larger than the male-female roles, it certainly includes that relationship. Peter confirmed this larger picture while noting the importance of a marital partner to the larger picture:

READ 1 Peter 3:1-7

1 Wives, likewise, be submissive to your own husbands, that even if some do not obey the word, they, without a word, may be won by the conduct of their wives, 2 when they observe your chaste conduct accompanied by fear. 3 Do not let your adornment be merely outward--arranging the hair, wearing gold, or putting on fine apparel-- 4 rather let it be the hidden person of the heart, with the incorruptible beauty of a gentle and quiet spirit, which is very precious in the sight of God. 5 For in this manner, in former times, the holy women who trusted in God also adorned themselves, being submissive to their own husbands, 6 as Sarah obeyed Abraham, calling him lord, whose daughters you are if you do good and are not afraid with any terror. 7 Husbands, likewise, dwell with them with understanding, giving honor to the wife, as to the weaker vessel, and as being heirs together of the grace of life, that your prayers may not be hindered.

In this passage Peter focuses on the importance of *submission* in marriage, particularly for the wife. This passage must be understood as part of the whole letter's teaching on Christian submission in all human relationships such as government (2:13-17) work (2:18) and at home (3:1). Christ is the ultimate example we follow in submission. (2:21-24).

Two aspects of the biblical marriage model are revealed by Peter:

1) Christian marriages may include an unbeliever, and the believer in such cases still has obligations of submission even to an unbelieving husband.

2) Husbands are to be understanding and to honor their wives so that their prayers will not be hindered.

READ: 1 Corinthians 7:2-5

2 Nevertheless, because of sexual immorality, let each man have his own wife, and let each woman have her own husband. 3 Let the husband render to his wife the affection due her, and likewise also the wife to her husband. 4 The wife does not have authority over her own body, but the husband does. And likewise the husband does not have authority over his own body, but the wife does. 5 Do not deprive one another except with consent for a time, that you may give yourselves to fasting and prayer; and come together again so that Satan does not tempt you because of your lack of self-control.

In this passage the apostle Paul responded to questions about certain issues in the Corinthian church regarding marital relations. He gives several principles of the model for Christian marriages.

First, one of the reasons for marriage is "because of (the threat of) sexual immorality", implying that marriages help avoid sexual immorality.

Second, the model of *each man* having his *own wife* confirms the monogamous aspect of marriage.

Third, the importance of sexual exclusiveness as a protection for the marriage is emphasized by focusing on active participation of both partners.

Like Peter's writings, Paul affirmed that a couple was *married* whether they were both believers or one was an unbeliever. He also acknowledges that the mixed couple has a special problem regarding *faithfulness to God* that must be managed to maintain their marriage.

Reading the entire letter of Paul to the Ephesian church would be helpful, but the following verses are very important in studying Biblical marriage.

READ Ephesians 5:21-33

1) *These instructions are written to believers, not unbelievers.* Certainly the guidance would be helpful to any marriage, but it is directed to Christians who are married to each other. Note especially 5:18-21. These are spirit filled individuals who speak to one another in psalms and hymns, singing spiritual songs. Both the husband and the wife were believers. However, the instruction is given in the context of revealing God's grand scheme for the world. *Christian marriages are the basic organizational units for the church as the bride of Christ.* This relationship indicates a special *spiritual purpose* for marriage.

2) *Wives are to submit to their husbands as the head while husbands are to love their wives with the same sacrificial love of Christ.* These two roles clearly reflect what was from the beginning in our definitions of marriage. Adam was first created, then Eve. Leadership authority was vested in the husband, as head. Husbands and wives have different but equally important roles.

3) *Marriage is an integral part of God's larger purpose in Christ for the world.* Paul emphasized that Christ was made to be head over *all things*. (Ephesians 1:21-23). This would certainly include a marriage where both husband and wife are believers but also one where one is a believer and the other is an unbeliever. God's larger purpose (even in marriage!) is the salvation of souls.

4) *Headship includes both nurturing love and authority.* What did Paul mean in Ephesians 1:22 when Christ is described as head? How does this help us understand how a husband is head? (Compare Ephesians 4:15.) Elsewhere the Apostle Paul says: *"Wives, submit to your own husbands, as is fitting in the Lord"*. (Colossians 3:18) In many ways the marital relationship models the divine relationship between Christ and God his Father! Submission means performing FAITHFULLY in the role assigned! Jesus was the Son of God with equality with God, but he was *faithful* unto death.

5) *The marriage relationship typifies how all things are brought together to become one in Christ.* In chapter four Paul outlines the oneness of the body of Christ. In Christ, in his body, salvation is found! This seems to imply that the institution of marriage is not an end in itself, but is a part of God's eternal plan for the redemption of mankind. Gary Thomas further expanded on this theme by quoting Dan Allender *et al* "Our marriages are the testing ground for God to win us to himself. Our marriages are basic training for the one marriage

that will not disappoint".[9]   That is, by making the
marriage relationship a "holy couple"!

Summary:

It is obvious that God's basic plan for marriage has
never changed! The New Testament passages cited show that
Jesus and the inspired writers Peter and Paul held to the same
basic plan:

A. Biblical marriage is a permanent commitment, a
   sexual partnership between a man and a woman.
B. The structure of biblical marriage is designed by God
   as the most effective partnership for training
   children.   Training children for the next generation
   is a powerful tool for maintaining God's image on
   earth.
C. Biblical marriage as an institution is protected by the
   sexual exclusiveness of the marital partners.

BOUNDARIES OF COMMITMENT

You might be thinking, "I know all *that* about *Marriage*! I
know about *Adam and Eve*! I understand that we planned to
be married *forever*! But...*it just didn't work out that way!*" Many
Christian fathers and mothers, including this author, argue
the fact that they have faithfully maintained their marriage,
taught their children the basics of marriage as described
above, and tried to the best of their abilities to live a good
example before their children. The sacred nature of biblical
marriage was taught and demonstrated, yet some of the
children's marriages did not withstand the assault of divorce.
The stark contrast of a loving biblical marriage and the ugly
destructiveness of divorce were evidenced in the same

extended family. How could this happen?

Now might be a good time to note some of the common causes of marriage failure. Divorce is a last ditch decision for a troubled marriage, so what causes a couple to call it quits? Researchers from the National Fatherhood Initiative conducted a survey asking people why they decided to untie the knot. Seventy-three percent (73%) of couples said a lack of commitment was the main reason their marriage didn't work. Here is the list as quoted by the Utah Commission on Marriage research:

1) lack of commitment (73% said this was a major reason).
2) too much arguing (56%),
3) infidelity (55%),
4) marrying too young (46%),
5) unrealistic expectations (45%),
6) lack of equality in the relationship (44%),
7) lack of preparation for marriage (41%), and
8) abuse (29%).

Perhaps it would be worthwhile for you to look this list over concerning your previous marriage. Other lists of "causes" or "reasons" for divorce indicate financial problems are the number one cause. You should understand that these lists record only what the individuals *said* was the cause of the divorce. In later chapters we will discuss many of these reasons in detail.

Marriage as a Legal Contract

Marriage is a legal contract traditionally defined between

a man and a woman by a licensed ceremony or a legal common law arrangement. A person is either married or *not* married according to the law. There is no legal status for engaged, or betrothed. Like any other legal document, marriage contracts contain small print which defines and explains the larger words of commitment in the document. In such an agreement, the two parties *contract* to an agreed-upon means of living together under law. This is usually thought of as a secular (this world) agreement, legally defined and regulated. Christians are commanded to obey the law of the land (Romans 13:1-4).

Marriage as a Sacred Covenant

But, marriage is also of divine origin (See Genesis 1-3), although it has been badly damaged and corrupted by sin. Sometimes the small print (*which may not be written down!*) and the intentional vows and promises a man and woman make with each other more clearly define the marital agreement than a legal document. Thus, there are two separate, but related, agreements in the marriage institution between a man and a woman:

1) First, a legal *contract* that binds two individuals to various psychological, social, and particularly economic laws of the land. These agreements are often contained in the licensing laws for the state in which the individuals live and where the contract is perfected. This contract *legalizes* a marriage.

2) Secondly, a *personal commitment* between a man and a woman wherein they promise, or commit, to each other various supportive and interactive benefits *in the*

presence of God and others. This part of the marriage agreement is usually couched in vows that are exchanged or *solemn promises* to perform a specified act or behave in a certain manner. God is not only a witness to the marriage, but a guiding force for how the marriage functions. These vows are usually considered sacred, not secular.

David Atkinson writes: "The primary purpose of marriage is to be found in the acceptance of God's will that the covenant relationship of man and wife, both made in the image of God, shall be an image of covenant relationship with his people"[10] This definition places the vows in a marriage alongside the vows we make with God. Whereas the *legal* contract marriage is heavily weighted toward society's standards, the *covenant* marriage is heavily weighted toward the spiritual standards of God.

Promises and vows form the core of the agreement between a man and woman who commit to each other in the permanent relationship of biblical marriage. These are based on two important passages of scripture, one in the Old Testament (Exodus 21:1-11, especially verse 10) and the other in the New Testament: (Ephesians 5:21-33), where "nourishes" and "cherishes" imply the provision of *food, clothing, and love.* These, along with sexual faithfulness, are vowed to each of the marital partners by the other. So *husbands ought to love their own wives as their own bodies; he who loves his wife loves himself. For no one ever hated his own flesh, but <u>nourishes</u> and <u>cherishes</u> it, just as the Lord does the church* (Ephesians 5:28-29). (More on "Vows" in the next chapter)

Commitment to God

Finally, *in defining the institution of Biblical marriage we must include the authority and power of God.* Christians are not just concerned about marriage as a legal contract or personal commitment to each other, but about how the relationship is viewed in the eyes of God. The vows that are exchanged and the promises that are made between a man and a woman under the umbrella of faith include God in the covenant. Marriage, instituted by God, is to provide the platform for doing the things of God in his created world. Gary Thomas reminds us that, *"The first purpose in marriage --beyond happiness, sexual expression, the bearing of children, companionship, mutual care and provision, or anything else -- is to please God."* [11]

Therefore we cannot clearly define marriage without restating this basic principle for all the saints: *"So, we make it our goal to please him"*. (2 Corinthians 5:9). We all want to be happy and satisfied in our relationships with our spouses, but *pleasing God* must be the guiding principle we follow in all things, including our definition of Biblical marriage.

Chapter 3

Man and Woman:

GOD KNEW HE NEEDED HER!

Seeker's Task #3: Re-affirm <u>how</u> biblical marriages work.

> *Your next task is to re-affirm the very heart of biblical marriage, the promises and vows. It is in these commitments where God framed a safe haven for personal risk. Your journey will take you back to the beginning when your marriage was in full bloom! This should bring back some fond memories, and be very helpful as you re-dig the foundations of marriage for the future. The goal of this task is to restore in your thinking the beauty and holiness God designed in the spiritual partnership of biblical marriage.*

Can you remember your wedding night? Sure, you were probably nervous and afraid! But, most of us think of our wedding nights as one of the most beautiful memorable times of our lives! The soft glow of the lights, a beautiful quiet room and maybe some soft music seemed to yell out: *THIS…is very special!* Biblical marriage *is* very special!

On the other hand, you may find this memory hard to think about because it brings up some painful memories and *sex*! Sex was at the least something you might have *avoided* talking about in your past marriage, and at the worse it was the major *battleground* that resulted in the demise of your marriage!

Single, *again* Christians who are striving to be super saints as suggested previously may also think it contradictory to complete *"Seeker's Task #3: Re-affirm how biblical marriages work!"* because you just don't want to think about *any marriage*. But this could be the best time for you to take a fresh look at *how* God planned intimacy in *biblical marriage*. Marriage was designed by God to be the most beautiful relationship between a man and woman. But more than that, marriage is a part of God's plan for His world. You are uniquely qualified to understand marriage *because* you are single, *again*. The fact is, your past experiences in marriage might have seriously skewed your views about this divine institution.

It may be far too early to think of remarriage, but if that is in your future it will be very helpful to clearly understand how biblical marriage is *supposed* to work! You might be vowing to yourself and others that you will never marry again because of your previous marriage experiences, whether they were good experiences or bad ones! This is even more reason to re-focus on the importance of *intimacy* in a *biblical marriage* designed by God. So, take off your blinders and begin to reaffirm the ideal pattern for biblical marriage as God *first* designed it.

First, you will think again about the promises and the vows you exchanged in the marriage ceremony. That's when you will probably well up with tears! Then the very misunderstood topic of "intimacy" in a biblical marriage will be viewed from a biblical perspective. It *is* about sex, but so much more. Finally, biblical marriage is designed by God for God's work in His world. Many married couples miss this point, but it is in marriage where we are blessed to *share in* deity! The very nature of the Godhead may be reflected in a husband and wife becoming "one flesh". But the procreation process, including making new life is nothing short of a divine miracle. This beautiful relationship is built on the promises of love and the vows of faithfulness typified *only* in a biblical marriage!

THE PROMISES OF LOVE

The relationship of a man and woman in *biblical* marriage is best defined as "intimate". That intimacy is based on a simple four letter word: L-O-V-E. Fred Lowery tells of a news organization that prepared a special presentation on "love" and "marriage". The reporters interviewed people from various cultures that practiced arranged marriages. Over and over the reporters heard the same thing: "You Americans fall in love and then marry. We marry and then fall in love".[12] "Love", regardless of the culture, is very important in defining how marriages work. Essentially, "love" defines how two people behave toward each other.

READ 1 Corinthians 13:1-13

This chapter is in the center of a letter written to a church with numerous problems. They were arguing and dividing. They disagreed on many things, not the least of which was marriage. Re-read this passage again and notice that when L-O-V-E operates it: *"suffers long and is kind; love does not envy; love does not parade itself, is not puffed up; does not behave rudely, does not seek its own, is not provoked, thinks no evil; does not rejoice in iniquity, but rejoices in the truth; bears all things, believes all things, hopes all things, endures all things.* Here is a clear picture of the kind of love in a marriage that will make it work!

READ Ephesians 5:21-33

There is no doubt but that "love" plays a major role between a husband and a wife. In fact, the Apostle Paul took it to the divine level by noting that this love is similar to the love that exists between Christ and his church: *"So husbands ought to **love** their own wives as their own bodies; he who loves his wife loves himself. For no one ever hated his own flesh, but nourishes and cherishes it, just as the Lord does the church"* (Ephesians 5:28-29).

Three Greek words are used in the Bible for "love": *"storge"* ("I like you"), *"phileo"* ("You are my friend") , and *"agape"* ("I love you unconditionally"). Unconditional *agape love* is the New Testament word for the kind of love God intended for biblical marriages. A fourth Greek word *"eros"* (sexual love), though not used in the Scriptures, is clearly significant in biblical marriages as well. The foundations of marriage are composed of a mixture of these four "l-o-v-e's"! However, it is not enough to simply say that biblical marriages are based on love! The love (or, *loves)* that make a marriage last for a lifetime are very complex.

"I Like You" *(Storge)*

It is very difficult to love someone you do not like. This word for love focuses on the companionship of a man and woman. In marriage the differences in each other as well as the things they hold in common mold two people into a *oneness.*

In the movie *Shenandoah*, young Sam asked Mr. Anderson (Jimmy Stewart) for his daughter's hand in marriage. "Why?"

Jimmy Stewart's character asked in his slow drawl! "Because I love her" was his response. "That's not good enough," Mr. Anderson replied. He went on to explain: "When I married Jenny's mother, I didn't love her; I liked her. I liked her a 'hole lot. I liked her for about three years after we were married and then it dawned on me I loved her. I still do. You see, Sam, when you love a woman without liking her, the nights can be long and cold, and contempt comes up with the sun."[13]

This is the kind of companionship in marriage that is celebrated. Two people live together, they suffer together, they learn together and they learn *to love* together! God knows and disapproves when His people do not always treat their mates with love: *"The Lord has been witness between you and the wife of your youth, with whom you have dealt treacherously; yet she is your companion and your wife by covenant."* (Malachi 2:14).

"You Are My Friend" (Phileo)

So much of marriage is about friendship. It is not unusual to hear a widow say at the death of her spouse, "He was my best friend". Marital love is designed by God to provide the unselfish dedication to another much like the love Christ has for us: *"No longer do I call you servants, for a servant does not know what his master is doing; but I have called you friends"* (John 15:15). A contemporary marriage and family therapist, after many research projects on marriage, stated: "The key to staying married is a beautifully simple concept with a profound impact: *friendship.* Happy and successful couples have a mutual respect for and enjoyment of each other's company."[14]

"I Love You Unconditionally" (Agape)

This word summarizes everything in the Bible about God's love. It is our model, our standard to measure the promises we make to each other in our marriage vows. It is the unselfish, self-giving unconditional love of God! This love in capsule form simply says, "God is love" (1 John 4:8). God's love is tenacious and everlasting. There is nothing you could ever do to stop God from loving you! God's forgiveness is conditional, but not His love! That's *agape love!* That's the kind of love biblical marriages are *made of! Agape* love *is* the very heart of made-in-heaven marriages. This love includes a commitment that will not be defeated. This is the love that remains when there is no good reason from the other person for it even to exist! With it you can start dancing in the rain when bad times come, rather than just trying to survive the storm!

"Sexual Love" (Eros)

Though the word is not used in the Bible, we express it in our love promises! Sexual love, or sexual intimacy is just *one part* of marital love, but it is so very important! Sexual love is the signature of commitment two people make with each other. Actually, *real intimacy* in a marriage occurs more from the neck up (our shared dreams and fears, our shared experiences, our unconditional acceptance) rather than from the neck down. But sexual love *is* the certifying act that binds us together as husband and wife. In a *biblical* marriage the sexual relations of *a* man and *a* woman represent the consummating act of their marriage. This physical union is sanctified by their promises of love. It seals their covenant together and binds each one to the other in exclusive privacy.

So, *can you remember* when you said, "I promise to love and cherish…"? Now, as a single, *again* Christian this word "love" may have taken on a different meaning. Nonetheless, Biblical marriage as God designed it is based on the very essence of God Himself –LOVE. Promises of love are of divine origin.

If God's trait of *agape* love is at the very heart of biblical marriage, then *His character* of faithfulness is the thing that holds it together! Faithfulness is fulfilled commitment. Faithfulness is the mother of trust. Faithfulness means to be strict or thorough in the performance of duty. One of my wife's favorite hymns is "Great is Thy Faithfulness" by Thomas Chisholm.

The chorus reads:

Great is Thy faithfulness! Great is Thy faithfulness!
Morning by morning new mercies I see;
All I have needed Thy hand hath provided -
Great is Thy faithfulness, Lord unto me!

VOWS OF FAITHFULNESS

One of the dominant traits of our God is His faithfulness. God keeps his word. He is dependable. We know we can trust him! He looks out for our back! That's also what faithfulness means in a marriage.

Your promise to be faithful was expressed publicly, and committed privately, in the form of vows. Your wedding vows were sacred commitments between you and your mate (*and God!*). You vowed to love each other and be committed to each other for life. These solemn words were probably sealed with the traditional phrase, *"...till death do us part"*! Even though there are some in our world who would change that phrase to "so long as we love", biblical marriages are patterned after the longsuffering never-ending faithfulness of God. When Christians marry they expect their marriages to last *"till death do us part".*

Sadly, if you are divorced, somebody broke his or her vows of faithfulness! It might have been an outright violation by sexual infidelity with all the ugly trappings that go with this ugly sin. Most divorced people, however, would simply say, "I don't love you anymore!" Probably lurking beneath the surface of the breakup were dozens of violations, sins of the marriage that do not end up on the legal documents as "the cause". These violations of vows are usually summarized in the phrase, "irreconcilable differences". Later we will remind you of what the scholars glean as Biblical grounds that can terminate a marriage. But for now, notice how the Bible defines "vows" in general and "marriage vows" in particular. These are the sentinel reminders that keep us faithful to a commitment.

A vow is a *solemn pledge,* a promise to perform an act, carry out an activity, or behave in a given way. There are about thirty biblical references to vows, most of which are from the Old Testament. For examples of biblical vows see Judges 11:30-31; 1 Samuel 1:11; Numbers 6:1-27.

How important is it to keep our word! Christians understand that a vow is a solemn pledge to keep our word. Solomon said, *"Do not be rash with your mouth, And let not your heart utter anything hastily before God. For God is in heaven, and you on earth; Therefore let your words be few.* (Eccl. 5:2). Jesus said, *"But I say to you that for every idle word men may speak, they will give account of it in the day of judgment.* (Matt. 12:36). According to the Bible, "our word" should be "our bond"! Vows are sacred commitments before God. They are given to be kept!

Bible Marriage Vows

There is no clear set of marriage vows recorded in the Old Testament; however, those who have studied traditional Jewish history[15] have found that the three components of Exodus 21:10-12 were typically observed: *"If he takes another wife, he shall not diminish her food, her clothing, and her marriage rights. And if he does not do these three for her, then she shall go out free, without paying money."* This close connection of the marriage vows to the right to divorce is evident in the Karaite-Judism tradition. These were back-to-the-Scriptures Jews of the seventh century who sought to restore marriage practices to the scriptural standards of the Old Testament. They concluded: *"He who says, "I refuse to feed and support my wife," must be compelled to divorce her and pay her the full amount of her marriage contract, as it is written, "He shall not diminish her food, raiment, and cohabitation. And if he do not fulfil these three for her, she shall go free."*[16]

According to these historians, the probable vows of faithfulness in the Old Testament made by the man committed him to provide three things for his wife: food, clothing, and conjugal (sexual) rights. He was expected to be faithful to his wife by providing these things. The wife, as the second party to the vows, was to be the wife exclusively for one man, her husband. Violations of the vows might free the wife to marry again or could cause her death!

For the closest thing to marriage vows in the New Testament read *Ephesians 5:25-31*. This passage compares the church of Christ to a marital relationship. The church is the "bride" and Christ is the "groom" who did everything for His church that any Jewish husband would do for his bride. The translations of *"nourishes"* and *"cherishes"* are congruent with other translations such as "feeding" and "warming as with a small child". The notion is that a good husband should commit to love his wife like he would love his own body: feeding, protecting and loving her!

Augustine considered the vows upon which a Christian marriage was based to be so important that they established a bond that was indestructible because of the sacred nature of the vows and the marriage the vows established. In other words, he believed that nothing could be done to break the marriage bond once the vows were exchanged.[17]

In the Sermon on the Mount, Jesus focused on sexual purity in marriage to affirm the unity and sanctity of the marriage relationship: *"But I say to you that whoever divorces his wife for any reason except sexual immorality causes her to commit adultery; and whoever marries a woman who is divorced commits adultery"* (Matthew 5:32). The Greco-Roman cultural world grossly corrupted marital faithfulness, especially for the woman. Men were free to have sexual intercourse with concubines and prostitutes, but the women had to live by different standards. Even the Jewish practices also devalued the role of the wife as the singular marriage sexual partner, allowing the men, under many circumstances, to have sexual relations with numerous women.

Thus, Jesus emphasized faithfulness over the more prevalent immorality of the age. Jesus taught that marriage was monogamous. Therefore any sexual intercourse outside of marriage was immoral and a violation of the marriage vows.

TWO SHALL BECOME ONE

In addition to promises of love and vows of faithfulness in a Biblical marriage the husband and wife are to " become one". The first sexually "coming together" in a marriage was described in terms like "(Adam and Eve) *became one flesh*" (Genesis 2:24-25) and "Adam *knew* Eve his wife and she conceived and bore Cain" (Genesis 4:1). Sexual interactions of husbands and wives are very important in God's plan. They also mark the boundaries of the partners' love and commitment. If you are single, *again* because of divorce, chances are you need a refresher course in *how* God designed two very different people to "*become one*".

READ Genesis 2:18-25

In the beginning, marriage solved man's problem of loneliness! Note in the preceding Scripture: "*And the Lord God said, "It is not good that man should be alone; I will make him a helper comparable to him*" (Genesis 2:18). God's plan for marriage was so that Adam would not be alone! Being alone, *single*, was "*not good*". Therefore, a part of becoming one flesh concerns the gender differences of males and females as a married couple. A larger part is the companionship, friendship and bonding-closeness the two individuals experience in becoming one. A state of marriage between two people is clearly preferable to living single in terms of loneliness and companionship! The prophet Malachi states: "*Because the Lord has been witness between you and the wife of your youth, With whom you have dealt treacherously; Yet she is your companion and your wife by covenant.* (Malachi 2:14)

The central idea of this passage is that the husband and wife are "companions" by "covenant". The wise man Solomon described an adulteress as one "*Who forsakes the companion of her youth, and forgets the covenant of her God*" (Proverbs 2:17). Biblical marriage is a companionship in which a male and female "commit" or "covenant" to be united *intimately* in daily living, thoughts, goals, plans, *and* physical bodies!

Thus, as we noted earlier in Chapter 2 (I Peter 3:1-7) God's desire for each of us is that we glorify Him. This can best be done in the gender opposite relationship of a male and female in marriage as designed by God.

Re-READ 1 Corinthians 7:2-5

Your journey in the previous chapter also outlined God's plan to protect a biblical marriage in three important ways: a) a commitment by one man and one woman for life provides marital stability, b). the importance of sexual activities in the marriage serves to help avoid sexual immorality outside of marriage, c). this sexual exclusiveness also required that both the husband and the wife be active participants in the sexual union. These are indications of how sexual relations impact the oneness of a biblical marriage.

> *Nevertheless, because of sexual immorality, let each man have his own wife, and let each woman have her own husband. Let the husband render to his wife the <u>affection due her</u>, and <u>likewise also the wife to her husband.</u> The wife does not have authority over her own body, but the husband does. And likewise the husband does not have authority over his own body, but the wife does. <u>Do not deprive one another</u> except with consent for a time, that you may give yourselves to fasting and prayer; and <u>come together again</u> so that Satan does not tempt you because of your lack of self-control.*

Now, in the same passage notice how sexual

exclusiveness makes the marriage *work*. Sex outside of marriage is *de facto* immoral. But also the model of *each man* having *his own wife* confirms the monogamous aspect of marriage. The core value that makes a marriage work is the love exchanged by the husband and wife in the private and protected structure of the marriage. The sexual exclusiveness of biblical marriage not only helps avoid sexual immorality, but it is one of the major tools in the marriage to produce the exclusive love that exists. Thus, husbands and wives are told *"do not deprive one another"* of this sexual privilege.

The denial of sexual intimacy can contribute to a person's spouse seeking the fulfillment of sexual needs outside of marriage, clearly defined as sexual immorality, though it does not excuse that sin. However, other personal sins and individual character traits and behaviors can also lead to unfaithfulness (See Chapters 5 and 6). One person's refusal to give or to accept forgiveness can also result in unfaithfulness (Chapter 7).

How Do Biblical Marriages work?

First, biblical marriages are formed because a man and a woman *commit to each other "promises of love"*. *Agape* "love" is patterned after the dominant trait of God, forever, unending, unconditional! The way two people behave with this type of love can be found in 1st Corinthians 13. This kind of love is the very heart of a biblical marriage. It is molded into the vows of commitment and sustains the relationship during hard times. These marriages are motivated by such love; and the husband and wife in the marriage behave according to the restraints of committed love. *Phileo* love (friendship) and *eros* love (sexual) are also lived out daily in the marital partnership.

Second, biblical marriages are held together by *the solemn commitment of faithfulness* engraved in the wedding vows. Faithfulness, like *agape* love, is also a core characteristic of God. The marriage relationship is formed publicly when two of them pledge to "nourish" (care for) and "cherish" (love) each other exclusively. The details of the commitment are couched in the Old Testament vows of "food, clothing and conjugal rights" (Exodus 21:10-2). The New Testament words that define that commitment are "nourish and cherish" (Ephesians 5:21-31) and "affection due" (sexual) each other (1 Corinthians 7:2-9).

Third, biblical marriage is the <u>only</u> relationship where sexual interactions between a man and a woman are good and acceptable to God. In the sexual act the created gender differences of man and woman are reflected in the very important traits of *headship* and *submissiveness* in marriage. We will later re-affirm these traits in the roles of husbands and wives. Gary Thomas introduced his chapter on becoming *"Sexual Saints"* by simply asking his readers the question: "Think of how God can reveal himself to you within your marriage through the gift of sexual pleasure?"[18] In marriage the sex act is where a man and a woman can <u>*literally*</u> act as God acted: *they act as creators to produce a new life*! This not only honors the exclusive sexual relations in marriage, but also makes sexual immorality a unique sin. *"Marriage is honorable among all, and the bed undefiled; but fornicators and adulterers God will judge."* (Hebrews 13:4).

MARITAL INTIMACY: A SPIRITUAL PARTNERSHIP

The Bible contains numerous examples of God using a pair as his basic unit. We all remember that two of each kind were saved by Noah in the Ark (Genesis 6:19). Jesus sent his early disciples out "two by two" to proclaim the Kingdom of God (Luke 9:1). In the final book of Revelation, God has "two witnesses" (Revelation 11) who are faithful to the testimony of God even unto death. In the beginning God created the ideal marriage of Adam and Eve as a twosome unit to act as one in taking dominion over the earth and to represent God.

God created this human institution of joining together *in His Image!* This is a powerful thought! Biblical marriage is not only of divine origin, but it continues to be God's basic unit for doing His work on earth! This thread runs throughout Scriptures comparing God's relationship to his people with the human institution of marriage. This basic structure in a biblical marriage also prepares both the husband and wife, but particularly the children, to trust and obey God.

In the beginning of time God made first the man, then from that man he made woman. Due to man *being alone*, God made woman to be his companion, a helpmeet. It was *not good* for man to be alone! The work that God had for this twosome-team was much more than just toiling to survive by providing food, clothing, shelter and conjugal rights. God intended for a man and a woman to be joined together and to work as a spiritual partnership with Him. The Apostle Paul called it a "great mystery" (Ephesians 5:32) when he compared it to Christ and His church. This mystery is best described in *how* God created male *and* female in His own image and placed them in position to care for His world (Genesis 1:27). Cleon Lyles, an Arkansas preacher, stated it the way God intended: "God knew he needed her!" Man was incomplete without the creation of woman and the subsequent union of marriage.

Chapter 4

Biblical Marriage:

CREATED IN HIS OWN IMAGE

Seeker's Task #4: Understand <u>why</u> God planned biblical marriage.

> *Previously you focused on <u>how</u> biblical marriages function in intimacy through the commitment to vows and promises between a man and a woman. Your next task is to understand <u>why</u> God created such a spiritual partnership. Biblical marriage is charged with doing the work of God on earth! This spiritual partnership displays the very image of God for all to see!*

Maltbie Babcock took his daily walk through a wooded area near his home in Lockport, New York. As he left the house he often said, "I am going to see my Father's world." In 1901 he penned the lyrics for the hymn, "This is My Father's World"[19]

Verse one proclaims:

> *This is my Father's world, and to my listening ears*
> *All nature sings, and round me rings the music of the spheres.*
> *This is my Father's world: I rest me in the thought*
> *Of rocks and trees, of skies and seas;*
> *His hand the wonders wrought.*

You have, I am sure, wondered at the Grand Canyon, or the majestic red woods, or the lofty peaks of the Rocky Mountains, or even less spectacular examples of God's world of nature! Absolutely breathtaking! The Psalmist says *"The heavens declare the glory of God and the firmament shows His handiwork."* (Psalms 19:1). You can see the hand of God in nature, our created world!

The created world around us calls each of us to the adoration and worship of our omnipotent and loving God! But, what about His *greatest* creation: MAN *and* WOMAN! The Psalmist described our creation as "a little lower than the angels" and that *it* (creation of man *and woman*) is "crowned with glory and honor"! (Psalms 8:3-5). In the previous chapter you were reminded that the first marriage between Adam and Eve was a result of their creation *in the image of God* God brought them together to reflect His image in His world. A biblical marriage projects the values, faithfulness, and very image of our Father in heaven. Though always less than perfect, God's traits are on display in such a marriage.

CREATION: GOD'S IMAGE ON DISPLAY

You can easily see God in the creation of His world. In nature we see his order and power. There is a constant give and take, ebb and flow that evolutionists have mistakenly theorized as organic evolution, without God. Christians see it as God continually displaying Himself, his power and his majesty! The creation of man and woman (and, the *Biblical marriage of the two*) was, up to then, the crowning example of God on display. Adam and Eve *was* the gender-opposite duo that actually became a *unit* prepared *by* God *for* God *to* represent God!

In the ancient East the erecting of the image or statute of a ruler signaled dominance over that region. Nebuchadnezzar, the King of Babylon *"made an image of gold, whose height was sixty cubits and its width six cubits. He set it up in the plain of Dura, in the province of Babylon."*(Daniel 3:1). He erected a golden statute that was more than ninety feet tall as *his image* to remind his people of who he was and what he represented. This erected *image* proclaimed the glory and power of Nebuchadnezzar.

Jesus was approached by his disciples about paying taxes, he responded: *"Show Me a denarius. Whose image and inscription does it have?" They answered and said, "Caesar's." And He said to them, "Render therefore to Caesar the things that are Caesar's, and to God the things that are God's"* (Luke 20:24-25). We understand that displaying the *image* of a person denotes honor, respect and even dominance. In this example, the *image* represented an obligation to be paid in taxes, a debt of homage to a governing power, the Roman government. That's important, but not nearly as important as the honor we pay to the very image of God as husbands and wives.

Biblical Marriage: God's Image

Remember the Bible description of the creation of the first man and woman: *"So God created man in His own image; in the image of God He created him; male and female He created them"* (Genesis 1:27). Like God's physical creation of the sun, moon, stars, and all that is on the earth, this twosome-one we call "biblical marriage" also reflects the glory and handiwork of God (Psalms 19:1). Man *and* woman! This complementary relationship, when uncorrupted by sin, displays the *very image of God* as creator, with His essence of love and faithfulness. This creation even included the god-like ability to create new life thru child-bearing.

Biblical marriage is not *really* the crowning display of God's image on the earth! Actually, *God's own Son Jesus was the exact image of God (I Corinthians 11:7)*. But, you might ask, how then does a marriage represent God's image?

Three designed components of marriage demonstrate *why* God chose biblical marriage as the basic unit for doing His work on earth. They are children, character formation, and Christ's church.

CHILDREN: REPLENISHING GOD'S IMAGE

Raising children to be holy! *Pro*-creation has come to mean having children. Biblical marriage is where a husband and wife come *to know* each other intimately. They enjoy the blessings of God while the love they have for each other certifies their union. Together, the wonderful power of creating a new soul in His own image becomes a reality. This power and the pleasures of their *sexual* intimacy are *protected* by their vows of faithfulness. That protected intimacy typically results in legitimately born children. The children born to this relationship come as blank tablets upon which their parents (*God's husband-wife team!*) write for them the components of a vibrant faith in their Creator! Brought up "in the nurture and admonition of the Lord" their children are made to be new images of God. Replicating *ourselves* continually replenishes the earth with God's images from one generation to another through *Godly families.* Seeing a Biblical marriage as God's basic unit for representing Himself on earth also makes bearing and training children of utmost importance.

A Family of God

READ Genesis 3:20-4:1

Biblical marriage is the joining of a man and woman according to God's laws of marriage. That marriage *usually* results in the birth of children. Then we typically speak of the Christian "family" composed of "mom, dad and the kids". Kostenberger defines a family as "primarily, one man and one woman united in matrimony (barring death of a spouse) plus (normally) natural or adopted children and, secondarily, any other persons related by blood"[20] This broader definition includes our extended family rather than just our biological family. The first family of Adam and Eve is described with two sons, Cain and Abel. The Bible says, *"Adam knew his wife Eve, and she conceived and bore a son, Cain…"*

In the Old Testament having children was a blessing, and to be barren was a curse. So, typically when a man and woman married the expectation for them was to bear children. This not only advanced God's physical world with more beings created in His image, but it also gave Adam and Eve the opportunity *to extend their influence through their children* to the next generation.

READ Deuteronomy 6:4-9

"Hear, O Israel: The Lord our God, the Lord is one! You shall love the Lord your God with all your heart, with all your soul, and with all your strength. "And these words which I command you today shall be in your heart. You shall teach them diligently to your children, and shall talk of them when you sit in your house, when you walk by the way, when you lie down, and when you rise up.

Biblical marriages are blessed to join God in *the very act* of creation by bearing children. There are, however, blessed opportunities and grave responsibilities indicated from this passage. Note the central theme in verse 5: *"You (parents) shall love the Lord your God with all your heart, with all your soul, with all your might"*. First, the married couple is to love God above all else. Their words and conduct are to reflect the "image of God". Then God says, *"you shall teach them diligently to your children"*. God's own image is transferred from one generation to the next as a husband and wife bear, raise, and teach their children to be like them…who are like God! Godly families, headed by godly husbands and wives, are on a mission to multiply God's image on the earth. Every biblical marriage is a new foundation for building that image.

Train Children

In such a marriage God is not only concerned with the couple bearing children but in training children to love God! Children in a Godly family are taught to obey (Ephesians 6:1) their parents in all things (Colossians 3:20). This is "Course 101" in learning how to be obedient to God. Children learn the basics from watching the daily interactions of husband/wife communications. The model for the parents might be reflected in the words of the Apostle to Timothy: "*but be an example of the believers in word, in conduct, in love, in spirit, in faith, in purity*" (1 Timothy 4:12). Show them what believers are supposed to look like!

God made this very intimate close private relationship of biblical marriage *the safe place* for giving birth to children *and* for training children. A relationship that is fenced in by vows of faithfulness and openly transparent in showing love! Then, when that intimacy produces offspring, children, God has not only a *safe haven* for them to grow and be nurtured; but also a most powerful teaching platform for the next generation!

For the Sake of the Children

Often in marriage counseling a couple contemplating divorce will defer it "for the sake of the children". No doubt children *can be* severely damaged emotionally by a divorce. We will discuss that later in our chapter on divorce. They can also be damaged spiritually as they observe the failed marital relationship of mom and dad. Children can be lost to God and his work because the parents did not perform their divine roles in the marriage!

READ 1 Corinthians 7:12-14

This Scripture is concerned with a mixed marriage of a believer (Christian) and an unbeliever (non-Christian). The unbeliever is threatening to "depart" or divorce. Paul indicates that it would be better if the marriage can be maintained. The believer certainly cannot sacrifice his or her faith to save the marriage. In addition, the children are "holy" and they must be considered in the matter. The unbeliever is allowed to *depart* (divorce) to keep the peace in the home. Why? Because one of the major purposes in being married is to produce children who will be taught to represent God in His world! Parents are created in the image of God and it is their responsibility to instill that image in their children. Paul's inspired admonition appears to release the believer from trying to maintain the marriage in such cases. Imagine an idol-worshipping husband and a godly Christian wife trying to agree on what the children are supposed to look like spiritually! It is difficult, and may not even be possible for a mixed marriage to raise *holy* children that are effective images of God!

CHARACTER: CREATING UNITY IN DIVERSITY

Building character from diversity! In a biblical marriage two very different individuals "become one". If gender differences of being male and female are not differences enough, each one also comes from a different background and culture. They might come with different problem-solving skills and even speak different languages. Just communicating with each other illustrates the issues common to diversity. In addition, both husband and wife are created equal but the husband is delegated by God to be the head (leader) and the wife is to submit (helpmeet). This divine structural relationship often creates problems with their distribution of power within the relationship. Yet as a husband-wife *team* they are charged with the task of caring for God's world and representing His image in that world!

Forming Character

In a Biblical marriage, when the two *really* become one with God, these diverse differences are unified by faithfulness and *agape* love through the process of their challenges and their successes. In such a marriage both the husband and the wife are humbled and *learns obedience* (submission) in much the same way as Christ and His Father are described in Philippians 2:7-8: *taking the form of a bondservant, and coming in the likeness of men. And being found in appearance as a man, He humbled Himself and became obedient to the point of death, even the death of the cross.*

Strangely, in our differences we *learn* to become one! But, more importantly this *give and take process* produces core Christian character traits in the husband, the wife, and the children. In a biblical marriage (or Christian *family*) the pressures of living together produces the traits needed to be effective images of Him in the world.

READ 1 Peter 3:1-12

Peter illustrates *why* and *how* biblical marriages can both make us holy and help us be happy! Gary Thomas asks a very important question: *"What if God designed marriage to make us holy more than to make us happy?"*[21] In this passage the marriage is composed of two very different individuals: a believing wife and an unbelieving husband. It is at the very heart of a theme that runs all the way through the book: *Christians are to be in submission!* In fact, he says we are to submit "to every human institution for the Lord's sake" (2:13). This included submission to government (2:13-17), to masters (2:18), and even to those who might harm us (2:19-21).

In this context of submission a biblical marriage is described between a believer and an unbeliever. The general principle that rules the believer's (the wife's) actions is be submissive to your own husbands (3:1). Why? That the unbeliever may be *won!* That the unbeliever may obey the Word and become a believer, a Christian! If you read further, and compare 1ˢᵗ Corinthians 7, it is also that the children may be "holy"! The goal is the same for all: *become His own image for all to see!*

How does that work? *"By the hidden person of the heart, with the incorruptible ornament of a gentle and quiet spirit"* (3:4)! This is a wonderfully powerful thought! A mate may be changed by the "hidden person" in all of us, our inner core character, our personal self! Not only is the unbeliever changed by the wife, but one would wonder where the wife got her "gentle and quiet spirit". Could it be from being "submissive" and from daily living with an "unbeliever"?

This passage of Scripture (1 Peter 3:1-12) should encourage every single, *again* person to prepare to be a super saint so you will not be "afraid with any terror" (3:6), even of being married to an unbeliever. A believer's best defense in the adversities of life is to be a *good* believer! Character matters, *period*!

This is one example of how the marital relationship produces character. While God's eternal plan is much larger than the male-female roles, these differences certainly impact a biblical marriage. Arguably, the most powerful one in this marriage is the wife. She develops a gentle and quiet spirit which actually *could change* the husband without speaking a word. We can only imagine what was happening to the children as they watched that wife/husband interaction. We can only imagine the tensions in this marriage as she submitted to her unbeliever husband. It had to be hard. But, like pure gold tried by the fire, the beauty of her character came out under pressure.

Forming Character takes Time!

But, becoming a clear *image-bearer* for God does not happen quickly. Christian character is formed over a long period of time from a wide diversity of experiences. That may be another reason why God planned marriages to last for a lifetime. Our parents lay the foundations for our core character but it becomes fully developed as we *intimately* embrace life as adults. Our mate is the most important person in our character-forming-process as adults.

Psychologists refer to this person as our "significant other", the one person in our lives who has the most influence over us! That influence is powerful if both mates are believers, but even if just one is a believer the other likely might become one by living with a believer.

Many modern-day marriages break up because one or both of the partners "just are not happy". It takes time for the myriad marital experiences with God to work the magic of Christian character-building! In any biblical marriage there will be good times and bad times. Some experts[22] would say it takes from nine to fourteen years of daily living this *give and take* process for a couple to create and form the oneness God designed in biblical marriage.

Holy Happy Marriages

Gary Thomas has outlined several spiritual goals God has for all of us that are more easily achieved by living in a marriage partnership[23]. Marriage teaches us to love, respect others, expose our sins, forgive, and to learn the power of perseverance. He further expanded on these themes by noting *"Our marriages are the testing ground for God to win us to himself. Our marriages are basic training for the one marriage that will not disappoint."*[24] This is a reference to being "married to Christ".

The best place on earth to stamp people with the image of God's character is in a family consisting of a believing husband and a believing wife working together with God in a biblical marriage. The core traits of God are showcased daily by the couple in such a marriage and transferred to the children. Thus, the children born to that marriage learn what it means to obey the "big guy"! The very image of God is made visible in the character of the godly mother and father on a daily basis. Then, the believing children grow up, leave home to marry another believer, to continue the character forming process to the next generation.

CHRIST: THE *IDEAL* IMAGE OF GOD

Faithful Christians represent God on earth! Jesus was the *actual* real express image of God on earth. He was Immanuel, God with us! Jesus was conceived by the Holy Spirit and born from the seed of a woman. He left us an example that we should be like Him! The modern day *real* images of God on earth are *faithful followers of Jesus!* In defining the Lord's church, the Bible uses the analogy of a marriage. Ironically, in the following passage the institution of biblical marriage is used to teach the truth about Christ and His church.

READ Ephesians 5:22-6:4

All the components of a biblical marriage (and Christian families) are contained in this reading: wives, husbands, head, submission, parents, children. But the key verse is v.32: *"This is a great mystery, but I speak concerning Christ and the church."* In this comparison Christ is the husband, the church He established is his bride (Matthew 16:18), and every follower of His are His children. Here the *ideal* perfect plan for His church and the *real* sinful men and women in that church who are saved by the blood of Christ are brought together! This passage brings us full-circle from what God designed for biblical marriage in the Genesis record and how sin changed it all. God intended for marriage to be an *ideal* working relationship with his crowning physical creation: man and woman. It was to be a divine relationship where God walked daily with his husband-wife team in the midst of His creation.

God's family on earth (His church) and the working relationships of a godly husbands (head) with good wives (submissive) and their obedient children represent the image of God to a lost world. The character of Christ, God's son, is the standard reflected. Many of the traits of God are mirrored in this *marriage/family/church* plan including love, respect, faithfulness, and even forgiveness from sin.

Next we will study biblical marriage and *divorce*. We will learn that even the best marriages can end in divorce because of sin. But first we should place God's ideal for Biblical marriage against the dark backdrop of what it became after sin entered the world. The remainder of this chapter is based on these basic principles of biblical marriage.

THE IDEAL BIBLICAL MARRIAGE MODEL

Summarizing a "Biblical Marriage Model" is very presumptive! The very purpose of our study indicates the complexities in defining biblical marriage and the confusion caused by making it simple. The three points that follow are *not* offered as an all-conclusive plan for marriage, divorce and remarriage, but simply as a general working outline for your search. What is obvious and "simple" is that God's *ideal* plan for marriage has not changed! The New Testament passages we will study later affirm that Jesus and the inspired apostles Peter and Paul held to the same basic plan outlined below.

However, the application of those principles to any specific marriage may be both difficult and different from one marriage to another. That is a matter for you to decide concerning your marriage of the past or possibly a remarriage in the future. Therefore, at the risk of over-simplification, the following three-point model is presented to form a general structure for your search to understand what God's will is for you.

1) One man and one woman: committed to each other for life

The biblical marriage model is a permanent <ins>*commitment*</ins> between one man and one woman who have vowed faithfulness to each other for life. Jesus said it was leaving father and mother and cleaving to a wife. This implied permanence for a lifetime. The Bible speaks of *a* husband and *a* wife in defining the structure of the marriage (Genesis 2; Matthew 5, 19).

2) Whose marriage is a spiritual partnership with God to do God's work on earth

Throughout this study we have emphasized that your task is always to do God's Will. The only reason you are reading this book, and taking this journey of faith, is because you want to be well-pleasing to God. The husband/wife team is charged to care for His creation, represent God's image on earth and raise children to do the same. The Apostle Peter (1 Peter 3) and the Apostle Paul (Ephesians 5) emphasized the spiritual aspects of marriage as the work of God on earth as God's representatives. Marriage was viewed by both as an important part of God's grand scheme of saving souls and glorifying God on earth.

3) **With exclusive sexual rights for both the husband and the wife**

The institution of Biblical marriage is *protected by sexual exclusiveness* for the marital partners (Review 1 Corinthians 7:1-9). To emphasize the importance of this protection, the penalty in the Old Testament for violating this sexual exclusiveness was death. Paul especially focused on the duties of husbands and wives as sexual partners. He clearly noted that a prime reason for the institution of marriage was to avoid sexual immorality. However, marriage also provides a safe, wholesome place for children to be raised in holiness.

It is not enough just to study the ideal model for biblical marriage. We should also note the abuses and corruptions that came in following the advent of sin. This search will also form a good background to study *divorce* in the next chapter.

BIBLICAL MARRIAGE CORRUPTED BY SIN

Soon after Adam and Eve were driven from the garden (Genesis 3), the *ideal* world became what we now know as the *real* world! Broken vows and sexual adulteries! The standards outlined previously did not change, but violations of those standards became rampant. Note the changes that occurred in marriages after Satan and sin destroyed the ideal biblical marriage. A cursory review of the abuses will certainly help us understand some of the issues surrounding divorce.

We are prone to think that the biblical standards were lowered when the violations occurred. The Old Testament is filled with examples of marriage failures, abuses, and other corruptions to the institution of marriage. However, the ideal pattern of God's design on any topic must be supported and defended even though individuals violate it. Yet, there is some comfort in knowing that some good people have fallen short of that standard. Abraham is known as "the father of the faithful", but he did not have an ideal biblical marriage. David was a "man after God's own heart", but he grossly violated the standard. Many Old Testament examples are both "encouraging" and "discomforting" at the same time! God's Word records the good, the bad, and the ugly!

IN CONCLUSION

Contrasting God's ideal plan with very real life situations described in both the Old and New Testaments can be helpful; but developing a vision of a good biblical marriage would be more helpful. Fred Lowery in his work on *Covenant Marriage* quotes Mike Mason who described what it meant each morning to wake up with a godly spiritual partner:

> "..it is with an expectancy of grace that I look over in the awakening light of this brand new day at the woman lying next to me, breathing lightly, like an organ of my own body. She is more beautiful to me than the light itself, more present than this towering mountain, her form under the covers is more elementary than any horizon, and she is closer to me than the air I breathe. She is "bone of my bones, and flesh of my flesh." There are other people in my life, but no one like her. More than anyone else on earth, more even than my own self, she represents the vessel into which I must and will be

poured. She will have all the very best, the cream, of my love. She is as close as anyone in the world can come to being for me, in that mournful radiant flesh of hers, what Christ is to me in the spirit."[25]

Chapter 5

Divorce:

WORSE THAN DEATH!

Seeker's Task #5: Don't Keep on Divorcing!

> *Seeker's task #5 will probably be a painful experience for you. It will probably be very sad, but maybe a little glad, too ...depending on your previous marriage! Here's the problem! Divorce, like a bad dream, keeps repeating itself! In this part of your seeker's journey you will try to determine what happened to bring about your divorce. Statistics indicate that you will remarry, rather than remain single. Also, the odds of you staying remarried are against you! Now is the time to take a critical look at divorce.*

In the previous chapter the first verse of Maltie Babcock's hymn "This is My Father's World" paints a pastoral picture of the beauties of God's world. When you married you probably stood before others and felt that same euphoria of happiness. The rose-colored world you imagined would include you and your chosen mate walking hand-in-hand as you grew old together! Your marriage was for life … *forever*! But, the third verse of that old hymn portends the reality you now face:

> *This is My Father's world, O let me ne'er forget*
> <u>*That though the wrong seems oft so strong, God is the ruler yet!*</u>
> *This is My Father's world, Why should my heart <u>be sad</u>?*
> *The Lord is King: Let heaven ring! God reigns: Let earth be glad!*

This verse outlines the theme of this chapter. It focuses on the two current realities of your marital life. In the first place, you must face the fact that you are single, *again* -- whether by an act of God (death) or an act of man (divorce). So, the *"wrong <u>does</u> seem oft so strong."* You are sad, and maybe confused. You have reviewed the ideal marriage plan of God and compared your previous marriage with it. If you are single, a*gain* by divorce you probably feel like a failure. Why shouldn't you feel sad and wronged!

But, the second fact in that hymn is just as real, *"God is the ruler yet!"* You are still within the sovereign power of a loving, forgiving God. You *yet* must seek His will and His guidance.

Your sadness being single, *again* could probably be expressed in the words of "Brenda" who, in a divorce roundtable discussion, said: "You're alone. I mean, you have your kids, and maybe you are blessed to have supportive parents who live nearby. Maybe you have some friends. But the truth is – *you are alone*! No matter how many people you know, no matter how many friends call you – *you are alone*. After you've been married a while, you get used to being "together" and you see your life as "together". All of a sudden, there is no more "together" –there is just you, all by yourself, alone. It is terrible."[26]

DIVORCE IS *REALLY* BAD!

The experience of divorce is *really* bad ...this you know quite well! However, the painful experience of a divorce may be necessary as the last resort for ending a really bad marriage. Losing your mate by death brings loneliness; but in most divorces the ugliness of anger, harsh words and cruel actions compound the hurt.

What do we mean by the term "divorce"? Divorce as applied to biblical marriage in this *Seeker's Guide* refers to the point at which a marriage is dissolved, ended! In such cases the individuals involved are no longer under bondage to the duties and restrictions of their previous covenant of marriage. By divorcing we mean a man and a woman have purposely and permanently separated, departed or divorced and have now entered the marital state of being single, *again.* Actually, how you define divorce will depend on how you define marriage. In either case, as a sensitive seeker after *biblical* marriage you will want to *know* whether or not your divorce was acceptable according to God's Word, or were you guilty of sin by divorcing. Whatever you determine, you will want to make sure you are right with God on the matter. That's what this search is about!

No matter how inexpensive the proceedings are or how necessary the split seems to be, divorce always comes at an excruciating cost. Financially, divorce often leads to poverty for all family members. Both spouses are often left with lasting emotional pain and regret. Some conflicts remain unresolved, allowing resentment to fester. Either spouse can experience anger, anxiety, depression and other emotions that affect them physically. The Family Values Institute (April, 2008) estimates that family fragmentation from divorce costs U.S. taxpayers at least $112 billion each and every year, or more than $1 trillion each decade.[27]

The effects of divorce on children are well known by both family researchers and the divorced parents of the children involved. In some ways this may be the highest price paid for divorce. What divorces cost children may be defined as:

- being insecure and afraid of the future,
- fearful of being abandoned,
- feelings of rejection, thinking they are to blame,
- feelings of powerlessness, torn in two between the two parents,
- being very sad and very lonely,
- stressed and highly anxious, angry and depressed.

Other potential risks to children include: poverty, mental illness, physical illness, infant mortality, lower educational attainment, juvenile delinquency, conduct disorders, adult criminality and early unwed parenthood.

Again, anyone who has gone through a divorce knows the hurts and sufferings that are inflicted on the husband, the wife *and* their children -- *plus* everyone else related to them!

Do you want to go through that again? Probably not! However, *beware*! Statistically, if you divorce once and marry again, the odds of you continuing to divorce increase tremendously. According to Jennifer Baker of the Forest Institute of Professional Psychology in Springfield, Missouri, 50% of first marriages, 67% of second and 74% of third marriages end in divorce.[28] Thus, you are much more likely to divorce after the first divorce than someone who has never divorced. A third "remarriage" is three times more likely to end in divorce! Sincere seekers of Biblical Marriage often *compound their problems* by <u>*continuing*</u> to marry and divorce! After a while, the depressing frustration of your spiritual well-being may appear hopeless! Many divorcees simply *give up* spiritually!

Becoming a successful Seeker will depend on three things: 1). Whether or not you learn from your previous experiences in marriage and divorce, and 2). By re-discovering and confirming God's will for you, and finally 3). Your success will depend on your ability and willingness, with God's help, to make changes in your life. These are the themes of the next three stops on your quest to *biblical marriage*.

DIVORCE! WHAT HAPPENED?

Divorce is *like* an accident. After the tragedy has happened and the victims have been given first aid and are transported into more intensive care, we try to solve the mystery of what actually happened. Details of the tragedy are important, but difficult to verify. The evidence from the accident scene is examined, including eye-witness accounts of those involved, circumstances of the situation, and likely hypotheses (guesses!) that might have caused it (the divorce) to happen. Like television *CSI investigators* we act as if we can know *for certainty* what caused the divorce!

Reconstructing any accident scene to determine cause involves the possibilities of two extremes. On the one hand there are victims who suffer more than their share of the troubles regardless of weather conditions, road conditions, laws violated, contemporary situations, and the other many complex components that caused the accident. Then, there are those who want to play god by immediately placing blame. This might include those in authority or those who especially were hurt because of the accident!

The problem is that a divorce *is not* just a typical car-wreck or other similar *accident*! It did not happen in a moment, but developed over time! The details of the action called a divorce were played out *mostly behind closed doors* over a long period of time*!* The best eye-witnesses are the two who divorced, but both of them are typically highly biased and emotionally charged. Each spins the story to meet his/her needs or to reflect to others what he/she thinks they want to hear. Often the one who speaks the loudest, or the most, is believed to *know for certain* what happened to cause the marriage to fail.

In addition, investigating the cause of a divorce by anyone outside the marriage is very difficult, if not impossible. However, everyone attempts to accept that role including the friends and relatives of the couple. Even their religious leaders feel duty-bound to determine *the* cause. Such attempts to determine the cause of a divorce by those outside the marriage usually end in faulty conclusions, damaging misguided advice, misplaced confidence, or the inflicting of additional pain and guilt on those of you who are now single, *again!*

That is *not to say* the "cause" (or causes!) of divorce are unknowable! Nor does it mean that what caused the divorce is unimportant. To the contrary, it is *very important* to know why a marriage failed ...*to the sincere seeker of biblical marriage!* That's the point: If anyone <u>*really needs to*</u> *know* why a marriage failed, it is the individuals involved...and God certainly knows! You, as one of the divorcees, should honestly seek out and determine what <u>*really*</u> caused your divorce!

In the remainder of this chapter we will explore some typical causes of divorce that come from the *common* sins of marriage. These are the things often heard in marital and family therapy sessions but seldom recorded in the legal documents. But more often than not, the little daily barbs of common sins become so painful that separation, hence divorce, seems to be the only option.

Then, in the next chapter our search will focus on other grounds for divorce based on passages from the Old and New Testaments. Our goal in listing the biblical passages with brief summaries of positions taken by theological writers is to stimulate further study to build your faith in God and His Word. We want to help you sort out your responsibility in deciding "What *really* happened" to cause your marriage to fail, and perhaps to prevent you from divorcing again.

Broken Vows and Promises

First, it is safe to say that in *any* divorce somebody violated his or her vows of faithfulness and promises of love. You both vowed to be faithful to each other "till death do us part". You promised your love "in sickness and in health". Such vows and promises are sacred and solemn. They are sacred because God is one of the parties to the marital covenant you formed. They are solemn, not frivolous or trite, *seriously important* because they affect so many people. We define a biblical marriage as *that which binds two people together in the intimate embrace of God's image with a commitment for life.* Such marriages are held together by the mutual commitment and faithfulness to the marital vows and promises. That's also God's outline for making a marriage work.

Obviously divorce changed all that for you. Very often by the time any divorce is granted, both the husband and the wife have violated their vows. Perhaps one may be considered more guilty or less innocent than the other, but actually the divorce might have been averted had you both *remembered* and *respected* your vows and promises! The Bible teaches that Christians are *required* to keep their vows (Ecclesiastes 5:2; Matthew 12:36). The *fact* of your divorce is evidence that *vows have been violated!* But, take heart, this exercise in reviewing divorce is to help you in the future, not to increase your guilt for divorcing. It is not our intention to make you feel worse, but to help you understand how to move on.

Modern Causes of Divorce

We could frame the problem of placing blame by just a cursory review of acceptable legal causes of divorce. Georgia, a southern "Bible-belt" state, lists nine legal causes of divorce: 1). Irretrievable breakdown, 2). mental incapacity or impotency at the time of the marriage, 3). fraud in obtaining the marriage, 4). adultery, 5). desertion for one year, 6). conviction of an offense involving moral turpitude and imprisonment for two or more years, 7). habitual intoxication or drug addiction, 8). cruel treatment, and 9). incurable mental illness.

In the state of Oklahoma those seeking divorce may elect to divorce on the grounds of "incompatibility" (No Fault) or on one of ten other grounds for divorce. These grounds include: impotence, adultery, abandonment for one year, imprisonment, confinement for incurable insanity for five years, cruel and inhuman treatment, fraud, if the wife was pregnant by another at the time of the marriage, gross neglect, or divorce in a foreign court.

The grounds for divorce for these two states are given as samples to show the diversity in divorce laws. Other states may have similar or very different grounds for divorce. The point is that we have legally tried to determine acceptable grounds (or, causes) for dissolving a marriage with divorce. The legal cause is important, but it is not always the *real* cause for the divorce. In addition, regardless of the laws of any state, you are more concerned with God's laws on the matter. That's is really important! How was *that* law violated? We want to be law-abiding citizens of both the world in which we live and in accordance with God's laws!

COMMON SINS OF MARRIAGE!

Actually, most divorces *happen* because of several reasons rather than one single cause. In counseling it is typical to hear summary statements like, "We just fell out of love", or "I'm just not happy". In counseling we call these statements "garbage trap" excuses. The two of them just dump all their frustrations, angers, and unhappiness into a single complaint statement that sounds respectable. The truth is that over a long period of time, perhaps many years, attitudes and actions fostered and promoted their eventual departure from each other. "We just grew apart" is probably a more correct conclusion, but no less destructive to the marriage.

It would probably be more honest to just say "What caused our divorce was sin!" But before your mind jumps to the scarlet sin of adultery, think about the other sins that might have wrecked your marriage. Infidelity *has been* identified as the most commonly _stated_ (not legal!) cause of divorce[5]. Sexual immorality does have a devastating effect on a marriage. But, other more common sins may have created the environment and provided the opportunities conducive to the adultery.

The lists of valid or invalid reasons for divorcing from research studies[28] are varied and long. One list includes general categories like affairs (27%), mid-life crisis (13%) family strains (18%), abuse (17%) and addiction (including workaholics) (12%). A more conventional list of causes might include money, communications, cheating, wrong expectations, commitment, sex, mid-life crisis, little things and society (easy divorce). Of course we have all heard of "irreconcilable differences" as the catch-all-say-all cause of divorce. This modern legal jargon may just be an expression of our frustrations in an attempt to isolate causes and place blame.

Sexual immorality was discussed in chapter 1 on the matter of "Living as a Super Single". There we learned that any sex outside of marriage is sinful. In the next chapter we will examine the Biblical records that depict the ugliness and damaging effects of this sin on a marriage. Sexual immorality is a BIG problem for any couple intent on having a biblical marriage.

But first we will discuss the more common sins of marriage which just as effectively terminate marriages and result in divorce. Some are either stated or implied from both the Old and New Testaments, while others are rooted in the personal characters of the individuals. These sins of marriage could fall into two categories: *sins in performing the relationship duties of marriage* and *personal sins of the individuals*. The failure of husbands and wives to perform the duties of marriage is a sin. God established marriage as a joint venture that involved specific roles for the husband and wife. In addition, any marriage brings two independent people together with, perhaps, different values and personal characters. For example, one might be a believer and the other an unbeliever (See 1 Corinthians 7). Individual sinful behaviors may have been taught and different character traits developed from their diverse backgrounds. Violations of relationship duties and personal sins are much more common in breaking up marriages than the graphic sin of adultery.

Relationship Sins

In a previous chapter we studied the roles and duties of husbands and wives in a marriage. These duties cluster around two sets of responsibilities divinely placed by God. First, they have duties to others as God's representatives (God's image) on earth to tend to God's business. Then, the husband and wife have marital duties to perform to each other. Finally, they together may have duties as parents to train their children. The Bible teaches that violations or neglect in performing these duties can be sinful.

The Bible defines the attitudes and actions of marital duties for a husband and a wife. In the following passage note how important submission is to that relationship.

READ Ephesians 5:21-33

Here Paul defines our duties to each other as Christians which cluster around the core duty of submission or faithful obedience to God. Just as Jesus obeyed the Father, we are commanded to develop an attitude of submission as well (Philippians 2:5-13). Thus, our husband/wife duties to each other in a marriage are defined in terms of submission, not pride or conceit. Arrogant behaviors are sinful in a marriage. In a Biblical marriage submission is the rule...*for both the husband and wife*! This not only includes the structure of the marriage (distribution of authority), but also the marital task of doing the Lord's work and representing Him on earth by submitting to God. It is in the intimate interactions between a husband and a wife that Christians learn very important lessons about serving God! Notice how important submission is for both the husband and the wife:

1) *"submitting to one another"* – This command calls both the husband and the wife to a covenant relationship *"in the fear of the Lord"*. You certified your commitment by the vows and promises you exchanged. That commitment included God-given-duties to be performed as a husband and wife team (a joint venture covenant!). Non-performance of your duties or abuse of your duties would be sinful. In addition, violations of marital duties might include sins against His church that are marital in nature. (See 1 Corinthians 5). Sins against the church that actually begin in the marriage might also include such things as gossip, causing division, slander and mocking.

2) "(wives) *submit to husbands*" - In an organizational way, wives are "to submit to" the husband. This command is congruent with 1st Corinthians 11:3 and Genesis 3:16 where the husband is stated to be the "head" over the wife. The implications of this duty for a wife beg the question of servant-hood and serving. Verbal and behavioral abuse, quarrelling and disrespect are sins that may result when the duty of submission is violated.

3) "(husbands) *love your wives*" – Husbands are to show their love by treating their wives as they would their own bodies. A husband is to "nourish" and "cherish" his wife (Ephesians 5:29) as the designated "head" (authority over) his wife. He must *provide* for her. When this command is violated, the common sins that follow might include harsh words, angry outbursts, and even physical and sexual abuse. Desertion would certainly be a sin depicting the failure of a husband to love and provide for his wife.

Training of Children

The training of children is a vital part of that spiritual partnership husbands and wives have with God. Christian parents are to "*train*" their children in the way they should go.

READ Ephesians 6:1-9 and Colossians 4:18-25

The Apostle Paul indicated that the presence of children added other duties (See 1st Corinthians 7). Thus, after stressing the importance of submission for husbands and wives the Apostle Paul invokes the same rule for children (6:1) and even for any servants in the household (6:5). Learning to submit *is* the core principle in living a faithful Christian life. Fathers are particularly charged to teach this principle as the leaders in the family. Thus, fathers are told to "*not provoke*" or to be "*harsh*" with their children. Physical abuse, lack of self-control, and other "power-related" sins may result when fathers fail in exercising their authority in a loving way.

Sexual Rights

The exclusive sexual rights in a marriage also are marital duties. A spiritually healthy sexual life between a husband and wife is a strong deterrent to sexual immorality as well.

Re-READ 1 Corinthians 7:1-5

Both the husband and the wife are commanded to provide the (sexual) affection due the other. Conjugal relations of a husband and wife are commanded by God. Essentially, Christians are told to "render" to their mates "what is due them" (sexually) as a husband or wife. The Apostle Paul commands by saying,

> *"Do not deprive one another except with consent for a time ...and come together again so that Satan does not tempt you because of your lack of self-control."* (7:5).

In summary, failures to perform or violations of the marital duties God entrusted to husbands and wives are sinful. In addition, many other common sins such as material and emotional abuse, neglect and even sexual immorality may erupt in these marriages. The structural interactions (submission and authority) and the personal communications (anger, quarreling, backbiting, etc.) also reflect the sinful acts of the marriage partners.

Individual Sins

At the same time, each individual in a marriage is personally accountable to God. These duties to God are individual and center on one basic value: being a faithful Christian. Individual faithfulness is reflected in the way we live, the behaviors we exhibit, and the overall example for good that we model in our character. (1st Timothy 4:11-16). Individually both the husband and the wife must be followers of God and walk in love. Neither can be guilty of fornication, covetousness, filthiness, foolish talking nor course joking. (See Ephesians 5:1-12).

Although the Apostle Paul shows the causes of the sinful conduct in the churches of Galatia by listing these works of the flesh, the basic principles apply to marriages as well. Whenever the works of the flesh dominate in any relationship devilish destruction will follow. In a marriage, that often is a painful divorce. Note how the New Living Translation states this:

> 19 When you follow the desires of your sinful nature, your lives will produce these evil results: *sexual immorality, impure thoughts, eagerness for lustful pleasure,* 20 idolatry, participation in demonic activities, *hostility, quarreling, jealousy, outbursts of anger, selfish ambition,* divisions, the feeling that everyone is wrong except those in your own little group, 21 envy, *drunkenness, wild parties, and other kinds of sin.* Let me tell you again, as I have before, that anyone living that sort of life will not inherit the Kingdom of God. (Galatians 5:19-21, New Living Translation)

These conduct disorders are among the common sins in many troubled marriages. Sexual sins are at the top of the list (including *impure thoughts* and *eagerness for lustful pleasures*) but more common sins of *hostility, quarreling, jealousy, outbursts of anger and selfish ambition* are just as damaging.

Relationship sins, marital sins, and personal sins are not suggested to be additional grounds for divorce. To the contrary, these sins may be just easier to correct than the sin of sexual immorality. Our purpose in listing them is to remind you that you cannot just keep doing the same things (common sins) and expect different results. If you are guilty of many of the marriage damaging sins in your previous marriage, you should make sure you correct them before divorcing again because of the same reasons.

Positively, you must demonstrate the fruit of the spirit. It _does_ make a difference in a marriage if the following traits are missing in one or both mates. The probability of divorce is greater when these character traits are missing:

> 22 But the fruit of the Spirit is *love, joy, peace, patience, kindness, goodness, faithfulness, 23 gentleness and self-control.* Against such things there is no law.24 Those who belong to Christ Jesus have crucified the sinful nature with its passions and desires.25 Since we live by the Spirit, let us keep in step with the Spirit. 26 Let us *not become conceited, provoking and envying each other.* (New International Version)

The Apostle Paul indicated that these sinful behaviors come from conceit or pride. (Galatians 5:26).

READ Romans 1:24-32 & 1 Corinthians 6:9-11

Consider the *most ugly* sins listed in the Bible, and you will be describing some of the common sins of too many marriages that end in divorce: vile passions, uncleanness, lusts of the heart, dishonor of our bodies, lies, sexual perversions, wickedness, covetousness, maliciousness, full of envy, strife, deceit, evil-mindedness, gossip, whisperers, backbiters, haters of God, violent, proud, boasters, inventors of evil things, disobedient to parents, undiscerning, untrustworthy, unloving, unforgiving, unmerciful, etc. (See Romans 1:24-32).

These sins, and others, are among the more common causes of divorce. Either the husband or the wife, or both, just do not fulfill their relationship duties to the marriage or one or both practice sinful behaviors. The marriage is often full of strife, unloving behaviors, and a lack of self-control. Such conduct is sinful. On the other hand, individual character flaws may result in chronic lying, evil-mindedness, fits of anger, jealousy, quarreling, lust and/or conceit. These common sins in any marriage will result in abuse and neglect. In some marriages, they even lead to violence! If left uncorrected, they are the sins that *actually* cause most divorces.

DIVORCE?! NO! GOD HATES IT!

Divorce is not something God intended "from the beginning". In fact, an oft-quoted Scripture plainly states that *"The Lord God of Israel says that He hates divorce, for it covers one's garments with violence"* (Malachi 3:16). Notwithstanding, God actually *divorced* Israel and threatened to divorce Judah (Jeremiah 3:1-20). Divorce did not originate with God, yet His servant Moses gave instructions regarding certificates of divorce. (Deuteronomy 24:1-4; Matthew 19:7). We have noticed already how that divorce is a costly painful experience for those who go through it! Yes, some marriages become so toxic and unsatisfactory that divorce seems to be the only solution.

This is when sensitive Christians ask the question: *"Is it lawful . . .to divorce . . .for just any reason?"* (Matthew 19:3). Some would answer: "No! It is _never_ lawful to divorce for _any reason_". In the current chapter we will review the most prevalent "no-divorce-for-any-cause" position that has traditionally been held in America. According to this view, it would not matter what *caused a* divorce simply because any divorce for any reason is sinful.

Other scholars would say, "Yes! You can divorce for _any_ _reason._ Most scholars see certain circumstances and exceptions as grounds for divorce based on the texts from the Old and New Testaments. These positions range from a single exception (sexual immorality) to several exceptions (desertion, abuse and neglect). We will study some of these positions in the next chapter.

No Divorce for Any Cause

The "No divorce for any reason" view on marriage and divorce, traditionally held by the Roman Catholic Church and some Protestant denominations, is simple: Once a couple is married in the eyes of God, that marriage is permanent and _cannot be ended_ by divorce for any reason, but only by death. While there is consensus that lifelong monogamous marriage is the ideal, there is no universal agreement among Bible-believing Christians on whether or not Scripture permits divorce and remarriage in certain circumstances.

READ Romans 7:1-4;

First, those who defend the "no-divorce-for-any-reason" position believe the position is taught by Romans 7:3:

"So then if, while her husband liveth, she be married to another man, she shall be called an adulteress: but if her husband be dead, she is free from that law; so that she is no adulteress, though she be married to another man."

Second, they cite the fact that no exceptions for divorce are given by the gospels of Mark or Luke, even though sexual immorality is the exception given in the gospel of Matthew (Matthew 5:32; 19:9).

"Whoever divorces his wife and marries another commits adultery

against her. And if a woman divorces her husband and marries another, she commits adultery." (Mark 10:11-12).

*"Whoever divorces his wife and marries another commits adultery; and whoever marries her who is divorced from her husband commits adultery (*Luke 16:18*).*

Third, the prevalent position taken by some of the early church fathers writing after the first century was that only death could end a marriage[29]. Here are two examples: "So that all who, by human law, are twice married, are in the eye of our Master, sinners."(Justin Martyr) "Now that the Scripture counsels marriage, and allows no release from the union, is expressly contained in the law." (Clement of Alexandria).

Fourth, the ideal nature of marriage described in Genesis 2:24 implies a lifelong relationship of the two who become one flesh. The term "one flesh" was typically used to refer to blood relatives., and could refer to the command in the beginning to "multiply and replenish" the earth, or child-bearing. However, the Apostle Paul used the term in reference to immoral relations with a prostitute (1st Corinthians 6:15-18). Illegitimate children would result from an invalid sexual encounter that was not a marriage. Thus marriage was to be a monogamous (eligible for child-producing) lifelong ("one flesh" always) relationship.

These reasons have led some to believe that there is no valid reason at all for divorce. This "No divorce for any cause" position is summarized in the following points by J. Carl Laney in his book, *The Divorce Myth*, (pp.91-102;103-114) as quoted in H. Wayne House (ed.) in *Four Christian Views:*[30]

1) The original creative intention and desired will of God is that marriage be permanent until death;

2) Neither God himself or God through Moses commanded divorce

3) The explanation the New Testament gives for allowing divorce in the Old Testament is the hardness of the people's hearts —hearts not submitted to the restraints of a high and holy God;

4) Paul asserts that the fundamental teachings of Jesus must be followed precisely, that the wife should not leave her husband and that the husband should not divorce his wife;

5) Remarriage is permissible without sin for a widow or widower, if the marriage is to another believer;

6) Remarriage following divorce, by either the husband or wife, constitutes an act of adultery;

7) Marriage to a divorced person constitutes an act of adultery;

8) When a divorce does occur, the only two scriptural options for the divorced persons are reconciliation or the single life.

Thus, according to this position biblical marriage can *never* be terminated by divorce but only by death because of the nature of the relationship. This view ultimately is based on the idea that when any marriage is valid and properly consummated before God, it *cannot be dissolved* by any man for any reason. Thus, to even discuss "biblical grounds" for divorce would be irrelevant! According to those who hold this view marriages can only end by death, regardless of the sins committed or the circumstances surrounding the marriage.

Religious Annulments

This has been the traditional position of the Roman Catholic Church with one caveat: *annulments*. Actually, an annulment is a legal determination that the marriage was never valid in the first place regardless of how long a couple has been "married" due to the very nature of marriage as a sacrament. However, the concept and the practice of giving *annulments* has been widely used to invalidate (end) marriages. The conventional wisdom of some would see an annulment even for a couple with children is in reality nothing more than a divorce by a different name.

Chapter 6

Divorce:

GOD'S *RIGHT* TO GIVE!

Seeker's Task #6: Confirm your faith in God and His Word

> *Your faith must be established on and maintained by a careful
> study of the Bible as God's Word. Make it your goal to
> understand God's mind on this topic, regardless of what others
> might say. Thus, seeker's task #6 is your opportunity to take a
> critical look at the passages of Scripture in which God interacts
> with those involved in divorce. Your task is to confirm your faith
> in God and His Word by understanding and accepting that under
> certain circumstances God does at least allows for and thus permits
> divorce.*

Divorce has become too easy in comparison with the
terrible harm that has been done by it. Getting a divorce has
become almost a national pastime in our modern world. In

America, approximately one divorce will occur (45.8%) for every marriage. Divorce is legally very easy! In 2001 a man in Dubai divorced his wife by a modern new method - he sent her a text message on her phone! She had failed to turn up on time to make his tea, so the man texted his wife: "You're late. I divorce you". This was the third time he had told her that he would divorce her, and according to Muslin law, it was legal and was later upheld by the Muslim courts[31] *Easy divorce*! One could argue that easy divorce is also a cause of the divorce rate escalation in America.

Yet, divorce *with* God's blessings, or at least with His toleration, is possible, according to some Christian authors! The premise of this *"Seeker's Guide"* is that: "Each Christian as a priest of God must discover *Biblical marriage* for him/herself!" We understand that God designed marriage from the beginning to be a lifelong relationship (Genesis 2:24; Matthew 19:3-9). But in the Old Testament and even in the first century divorce was a reality of life. Just as you must determine for yourself the validity of your marriage, you also must determine the validity of your divorce, and perhaps later, the validity of remarriage. You will want to know under what conditions, or circumstances, do you have God's permission to end your marriage by divorce.

"ALLOWABLE" GROUNDS FOR DIVORCE

We assume you want to please God. Anything that others, including religious leaders, might say cannot make a marriage that is *acceptable* to God unacceptable! By the same argument if a person is divorced on grounds that are *allowed* by God, no man can speak evil of it. *"Allowable grounds* for divorce" include what some scholars say are grounds for divorce that would be acceptable to God. You must determine what are valid grounds based on the conclusions you draw from God's Word *and* the situation of your own divorce!

Why would you want to know whether or not your divorce was according to what God allows? Very simple! If your divorce was on grounds allowed in the scriptures, you did not sin by getting a divorce. On the other hand, if your divorce came about for other reasons, you have violated the laws of God and are guilty of sin. How you move forward into the future if you had *not sinned* is very different from what you must do if you *had sinned!* Briefly stated, repentance is essential to correct a sin, whereas if no sin was committed repentance is not required. We will discuss this in more detail in Chapter 8 on *Spiritual Recovery and Repentance.* The fact is, some writers believe that any divorce is sinful.[32] If that is the case, then any divorce will require repentance. As a sincere seeker you have one goal: "…you ought to walk and to please God" (I Thessalonians 4:1)

However, having said that, *it is valuable* in your search to understand the various positions, commentaries, and theological attempts to define God's "grounds" (allowable reasons) for divorce based on the Bible. These biblical grounds form the basis upon which God gives you permission to divorce and remain acceptable to Him.

The most commonly used biblical passages that pertain to divorce will be presented. Read them for yourself in *your* Bible. This will help you sort out your responsibilities in deciding "What happened to cause my divorce?" and "Was my divorce with God's permission?" The answers to both these questions are important for your spiritual health. But, remember only you and God can *truly* know the data for the answers to these two questions.

Christians must ultimately define any permissible divorce position on the teachings and standards of the New Testament, rather than the Old Testament. However, the Apostle Paul stated *"for whatever things were **written** before were **written for our learning**, that we through the patience and comfort* *of the Scriptures might have hope"* (Romans 15:4 NKJV). Old Testament passages regarding divorce will help us understand the mind of God. Thus, before we study the key passages in the New Testament we will bookmark Old Testament passages pertaining to divorce, including the passage quoted by Matthew.

Old Testament on Divorce

READ Ezra 9-10

Suffice it to say, God "hates divorce" because He has been involved in it! In a metaphoric way the Old Testament records demonstrate how God divorced Israel and threatened to divorce Judah, "her sister" for "unfaithfulness" (See Ezekiel 23:9-33; Malachi 2:10-16). In Ezra 9-10, God sanctions a mass divorce of Jewish men who had married foreign women. These passages, and others in the Old Testament, will be studied later under "Divorce for Covenant-Breaking", which included sexual unfaithfulness.

READ Hosea 1-3

The Old Testament example of Hosea's divorce from his wife Gomer (Hosea 1-3) confounds our understanding of Old Testament grounds for divorce. If anyone had a valid "cause" for divorce due to "sexual immorality" it was Hosea! *...his wife (Gomer) was repeatedly sexually unfaithful!* But, Hosea accepted her back even after she "played the prostitute"! This example also reflects God's forgiving attitude toward his unfaithful people. He would have gladly accepted them back if they had repented and returned.

READ Deuteronomy 22:13-29

In this Old Testament passage are two examples in

which a man _was prohibited_ from divorcing his wife. Both cases involved sexual relations with a virgin. In the first case a man took a wife and then charged her with "shameful conduct", that of not being a virgin. The second case was of a man who seized a "non-betrothed" virgin and had sexual relations with her. In both cases "he shall not be permitted to divorce her all his days" (Deuteronomy 22:19,29).

By reading the entire passage you should note that there were differences in the way God viewed the situations *based on the circumstances involved* such as whether the event occurred "in the country" or "in the city" or whether or not the virgin protested by "calling out".

In the first example of "no divorce for any reason" a man took a wife and then charged her with "shameful conduct", that is, of not "being a virgin" when he married her (22:13-14). The charge implied that she had had sexual relations prior to their marriage. Like adultery, this was an accusation against the virgin's father. Therefore, the father of the woman defended her virginity before the elders and proved that she was unlawfully charged. (vss. 15-17). The man who had married her and then accused her of the shameful conduct (essentially, sexual immorality) was fined one hundred shekels of silver to be *paid to the father*. More important, the man *"could not divorce her all his days"* (vs. 19).

The second example is about a man who had pre-marital sex with a virgin *who was not betrothed (engaged to be married)*, and they are "found out" (22:28-29). The man was required to take her for his wife and was *"not permitted to divorce her all his days"* (vs. 29). In this case the father of the young woman must be paid fifty shekels of silver as penalty. Half of what was required in the first example!

The prescribed penalty for all sexual immorality resulted in the individuals involved being stoned to death. (Leviticus

20:10-13). Illicit sexual relations in this passage with virgins or with other men's wives constituted sexual immorality.

The silence of the scriptures might suggest that since there were *only two* examples in which a man *could not* divorce his wife for any circumstance would suggest that there were other situations in which a man could, with God's permission, divorce his wife. Divorces were probably more common in the Old Testament than most of us want to admit. Divorce, like many other human institutions, came after sin entered the world. God's ideal plan for marriage, as noted earlier, was for a lifelong covenant relationship in which a man and a woman were teamed-up to tend God's world. Divorce came later after the fall of man into sin. However, the Old Testament does include examples and regulations for divorce.

READ Deuteronomy 24:1-4

We will revisit this passage later in the course of studying Jesus' encounter with the Pharisees (Matthew 19:3-10). This is the first passage in the Bible that notes a "cause" for divorce. Read the passage again noting our *emphasized* words:

"When a <u>man</u> takes a wife and marries her, and it happens that <u>she finds no favor</u> in his eyes because <u>he has found some uncleanness in her</u>, and he writes her a certificate of <u>divorce</u>, puts it in her hand, and sends her out of his house, 2 when she has departed from his house, and goes and becomes another man's wife, (remarriage) *3 if the latter husband <u>detests her</u> and writes her <u>a certificate of divorce</u>,* (second marriage, second divorce) *puts it in her hand, and sends her out of his house, or if the latter husband dies who took her as his wife, 4 then her former husband who divorced her <u>must not take her back to be his wife</u> after she has been defiled; for that is an abomination before the Lord,*

The following points may be noted in this Old Testament passage:

A valid marriage was dissolved by divorce on the grounds of "uncleanness".

1) The divorced wife became another man's wife.
2) The divorced wife was divorced a second time or the husband died.
3) The first husband could not remarry the previously divorced wife.

It is of interest at this time to consider the cause of the divorce in this passage. What was the cause of the woman's first divorce? It is stated by various translations as *"finds no favor in his eyes"* (because) of some *"uncleanness"*(NKJV), *"discovers something about her that is shameful"* (NLT), or (finds) *"some indecency about her"* (RSV).

In the previous text "shameful conduct" was the "cause" that the man used to "send his wife away" (Deuteronomy 22:13-29). He claimed that she was not a virgin when he married her, meaning that she had been guilty of sexual immorality, pre-marital sex. Sexual immorality in the Old Testament included pre-marital sex, sex with another man's wife, and perhaps (based on the penalties prescribed) incest, homosexual sex, sex with animals and fornication (Leviticus 18:1-30). The prescribed penalty for such "sexual immorality" was that the individuals were to be *stoned to death*, or *cut off from the people* (Leviticus 20:10-21).

Divorce in the New Testament

Our information about the topic in the New Testament comes from passages where Jesus was confronted by the Pharisees in the gospel records and from passages where the Apostle Paul expands on the topic for the Corinthian church. First, study the words of Jesus.

READ Matthew 19:3-10; Mark 10:1-12

The key verse in this passage is:

And I say to you, whoever divorces his wife <u>except for sexual immorality</u>, and marries another, commits adultery; and whoever marries her who is divorced commits adultery"(Matthew 19:9).

Matthew's account of the dialogue between Jesus and the Pharisees in the following text inserts "sexual immorality" (NKJV) as the single exception for allowable divorce. Neither the gospel account of Mark (10:11-2) nor of Luke (16:18) includes this exception. Matthew also includes sexual immorality as an exception for divorce in the Sermon on the Mount in Matthew 5:31-32. We will also study this passage in conjunction with other views later.

Many believe the discussion between Jesus and the Pharisees pertains to Deuteronomy 24. The Jewish schools of Shammai and Hillel were hotly debating these issues at the time Christ was tested in Matthew19. The followers of Hillel focused on the "cause" of *"finds no favor in his eyes"* to mean divorce for "any cause", or "any matter". The followers of Shammai focused on the *"some uncleanness"* issue which they interpreted to mean any sexual impurity as defined in Leviticus and Deuteronomy. The Hillel school would argue that only a sexual matter could be used for issuing a certificate of divorce. Whereas the school of Shammai would include "any matter", assuming it was a valid Biblical cause. The more permissive position (Hillel, "any matter") was the prevailing teaching of the rabbis during the days of Christ. (For a thorough discussion of Deuteronomy 24:1-4, See Instone-Brewer).[33]

In this encounter the Pharisees were testing Jesus about what has been called the "Mosaic toleration," a divorce policy based on Deuteronomy 24 enacted by God to regulate divorce. Since only men could initiate a divorce, the "Mosaic toleration" appeared to be a protection for women.

Why did you Divorce?

This part of your journey can be difficult and very confusing because there are about as many stated *biblical grounds for divorce* as there are writers! In addition to that, you will need to consider some arguments from human reasoning. Sometimes "the grounds for divorce" arguments hang on the original meanings of Bible language words, which in translation can seem to be contradictory and are often tedious to study. The purposes of this book do not include such detailed analysis, but provide a general review of various positions. You can extend your study by going to the original works listed in Resources in the back of the book . Volumes are in print on each of these views. They were written by authors who, like you, sincerely want to please God. This is simply a *guide* for _your_ study *not a treatise to convince you* whether or not your divorce is acceptable or unacceptable to God.

We will be as fair as we can in presenting the views, but our bias for one position over another will likely be evident. However, we do not want to speak where the Bible *does not* speak! Many of the positions on divorce and remarriage tend to be based on human reason, or subjective conclusions, or to go beyond what is written in God's Word. We do, however acknowledge that valid conclusions can be drawn from the silence of the Scriptures.

Biblical "Allowable" Causes

We have grouped the various "allowable" causes for divorce into four general positions to help you organize your search. The word "allowable" is placed in quotes to indicate that we are presenting positions held by others, not necessarily positions we believe or that you should adopt. You will have to do your own homework to determine which of these positions would be God's position.

Thus, for the sake of organization, here are four general categories of causes put forth to be the truth on the matter:

1) Divorce for Sexual Immorality Only
2) Divorce for Desertion in Spiritually Mixed Marriages
3) Divorce for Abuse and/or Neglect
4) Divorce for Covenant-breaking

There are also differing views within each general position on some specific detail or special circumstance. For example, within the "Sexual Immorality Only" view one writer may disagree with another writer on the definition of "adultery"; whether it is "any act of sex" or "only sex between two married individuals". In addition, many challenging questions are raised for all the "exceptions". For example, "Is internet pornography or chronic lust equivalent to adultery? Or, "Is there a significance to *when* a person seeks a divorce after a biblical cause has been committed?"

These brief summaries do not fully present the views of the scholars quoted. In addition, there is a general consensus among the scholars that individuals should strive to maintain their marriages. The generally accepted belief is that marriages are instituted by God, and therefore no one should take the dissolution of a marriage lightly! As a careful seeker you will want to read the primary sources on the various positions before forming your conclusions.

DIVORCE FOR SEXUAL IMMORALITY ONLY

If no divorce for any cause is the traditional Catholic position, divorce for sexual immorality only is the prevailing Protestant view[34]. This position, or variations of it, is also the traditional view of the majority of writers in restoration churches of Christ.[35] Schubert states, "*The teaching is plain. There is one and only one scriptural cause that can justify divorce and remarriage, and this cause is fornication*"[36] Those who hold this position base their understanding on Matthew's account of a testing between Jesus and the Pharisees (Matthew 19:3-12) about "Is it lawful for a man to divorce his wife for just any reason?" This issue was probably based on the debate over an Old Testament passage, Deuteronomy 24:1-4.

The "sexual immorality only" position could be viewed as an extension or amendment to the position of "No Divorce". In the "no divorce" view, to divorce for any cause would be a sin; in the extension, to divorce for any cause *other than fornication* would be a sin! Both positions depend on a clear definition of biblical marriage. In the "sexual immorality only" view there must also be a documented and proven case of sexual immorality (or, uncleanness).

If sexual immorality is the one biblical cause for divorce, then that cause must not only be *clearly defined* but there must also be ample evidence that it actually has occurred. For example, is it possible for a person to "commit adultery in his heart" What about pornography? How would you consider sexual crimes such as homosexuality, incest or bestiality? Sexual immorality is difficult to define and more difficult to legally prove. For these reasons "sexual immorality" is seldom written on the divorce documents as the cause of the divorce, even though it may have actually occurred!

Adultery (sexual infidelity) was very serious in Bible days and could be punishable by death, although the penalty of death was rarely administered. No one should doubt the destructive impact of this sin on a marriage. Paul said it clearly,

> "Flee sexual immorality. Every sin that a man does is outside the body, but he who commits sexual immorality sins against his own body. Or do you not know that your body is the temple of the Holy Spirit who is in you, whom you have from God, and you are not your own? For you were bought at a price; therefore glorify God in

your body and in your spirit, which are God's. (1 Corinthians 6:18-20).

Make no mistake about it: unfaithfulness due to sexual infidelity is a uniquely destructive sin in any marriage. It is the most prevalent *official* Christian view for divorce taken by fundamentally conservative churches. Sexual immorality is diametrically opposed to the purity and holiness expected of such believers.

DIVORCE FOR DESERTION

Others hold the position that divorce is allowed by God in cases of abandonment, or if one partner just departs and deserts the marriage. This view is based on the teachings of the Apostle Paul to the church that was planted in the pagan city of Corinth. The marriage in the passage under review, however, is a spiritually mixed marriage of a "believer" and an "unbeliever", possibly a pagan-worshipping partner married to a mate who had become a Christian. If a (pagan) husband or (pagan) wife "is unwilling to live with" the believer, then "let them depart".

READ 1ˢᵗ Corinthians 7:12-16

12 But to the rest I, not the Lord, say: If any brother has a wife who does not believe, and she is willing to live with him, let him not divorce her. 13 And a woman who has a husband who does not believe, if he is willing to live with her, let her not divorce him. 14 For the unbelieving husband is sanctified by the wife, and the unbelieving wife is sanctified by the husband; otherwise your children would be unclean, but now they are holy. 15 But if the unbeliever departs, let him depart; a brother or a sister is not under bondage in such cases. But God has called us to peace. 16 For how do you know, O wife, whether you will save your husband? Or how do you know, O husband, whether you will save your wife?

Reconciliation, or maintaining the marriage is again stated as the most desirable option for any marriage. Christians should strive to "remain in the state" in which they are called. (7:20). However, according to some writers "spiritual incompatibility" can be acceptable grounds for divorce.[37] In this context if an unbeliever departs and is unwilling to live with the believer, the believer is to "let them depart". The indication is that the marriage is conflicted due to the spiritual differences between the husband and wife. Their marriage may be characterized by daily conflict over their different religious views.

This passage contains several points that are the focus of controversy by theological writers. The phrase "*I, not the Lord*" (7:12) indicates that this instruction was either different from what was taught by Jesus or was an extension of what was taught by Jesus. In verse 10 Paul stated that "*the Lord*" said a wife should "*not depart*". Jesus was perhaps speaking about marriages where both were Jews, living under the Mosaic laws. Paul was instructing the church in Corinth about marriages where one was a Christian and the other a pagan. In this context the Bible describes a marriage stressed by spiritual and religious differences of the couple.

The important point for you to consider as a single, *again* Christian is whether or not grounds for permissible divorce are given by the Apostle Paul *in addition* to what was given by Jesus in Matthew's account? Additionally, is divorce allowed for desertion by an *unbeliever*, but not allowed if the *believer* departs? How broadly is "spiritual incompatibility" defined? More generally, if this passage allows for divorce for *the stated circumstances* (believers married to unbelievers) is it possible that other similar, or even dissimilar circumstances might also allow divorce? For example some would argue, "*If you and your children are at risk because of his drug use or abusive behaviors, "departing" may be necessary in order to protect yourselves from the immediate or long-term harm he is inflicting on you.*"[38]

Important principles are implied in this passage for the institution of marriage. Man and woman (in marriage) are created in the image of God and entrusted with the task of doing the business of God. (See Chapter 4). Consider these questions in deciding either to maintain the marriage or to seek a divorce:

1. *What impact will staying in the marriage or divorcing have on the children and their salvation (7:14)?*
2. *What are the possibilities that the unbeliever will be saved(7:16)?*
3. *How can peace be experienced in the marriage (7:15)?*

READ 1st Corinthians 7:1-5

A mate may deprive the other mate regarding his or her conjugal duties as a husband or wife. In this context the Apostle Paul confirms the spiritual dignity of sexual relations between a man and woman married to each other. The instruction is clear: *"do not deprive one another except with consent for a time"* (7:5) and then *"come together again"* (referring to sexual activity). The reason was stated earlier, *"because of sexual immorality"* (7:2). In short, it is the conjugal duty of both the husband and the wife to participate in the sexual union within the marriage. This, among other things, makes them *"one flesh"* (Genesis 2:24-25; Matthew 19:5). This command for sexual involvement by the husband and wife may also deter sexual immorality, as has already been stated.

Obviously, the marital duties cannot be fulfilled by a husband or wife who has "departed". One might argue about the amount of time required for such abandonment to become a valid reason to end a marriage. Would a long weekend of drunken stupor be abandonment? Or, must the abandoned spouse wait years! Either way, the possibility of such a violation is implied.

DIVORCE FOR ABUSE AND NEGLECT

A third general category of biblical grounds for divorce suggested by the literature focuses on abuse and neglect. No doubt both sexual unfaithfulness and desertion could also be defined as marital abuse or neglect in any divorce proceedings.

READ Exodus 21:10-11

If he takes another wife, he shall not diminish her <u>food</u>, her <u>clothing</u>, and her <u>marriage rights</u>. And if he does not do these three for her, then she shall go out free, without paying money.

These three provisions in a marriage (food, clothing, marriage rights) were usually defined under two headings by the rabbis when in a divorce proceeding: *material neglect* and *emotional abuse*. This text is rarely used to discuss marriage and divorce but a wife was clearly "set free" (divorced) by the husband in this passage. In fact, Instone-Brewer[39] believes our modern marriage vows are based directly on this passage and the words of the Apostle Paul:

READ Ephesians 5:28-29

28 So husbands ought to <u>love</u> their own wives as their own bodies; he who loves his wife loves himself. 29 For no one ever hated his own flesh, but <u>nourishes and cherishes</u> it, just as the Lord does the church.

According to this position a failure to "nourish and cherish" (feed and keep warm) would be "material neglect" while a violation of the vow "to love" would be deprivation of conjugal rights[40].

The instructions in Exodus 21:10-11 pertain to a slave wife or concubine. It is assumed that the same rights for a concubine to *"go free"* would certainly apply to any other wife who was not taken as a slave. The question is: "What violations of the marital covenant are required for her husband to let her "go free" or depart?" The answer is that if the husband does not properly a). provide her food, b). her clothing, and c). her conjugal (sexual) rights then she may "go out free".   The entire transaction is seen as a marital issue since the stipulation is added that the departing (divorce) does not require paying money. Wives were generally obtained by marriage payments, a bride price (a *ketubah)*, to the father of the bride (Genesis 34:11-12; 1 Samuel 18:25). This generally went with the bride if she were to be divorced. The fact that this is even mentioned indicates that this was considered a marriage.

This passage also indicates that the marriage vows written into the marital covenant of the Old Testament centered around these three provisions: food, clothing, and the sexual relations between the husband and wife. Failure to provide these marital duties was defined as physical and/or emotional abuse. These three "provisions" were universally accepted as grounds for divorce throughout the Old Testament and into the time of Christ.[41]   Shelly observes that this might help explain another Old Testament example of how Abraham was reluctant to send Hagar, his slave wife away [42]

DIVORCE FOR COVENANT-BREAKING

The fourth general category for "Allowable Causes for Divorce" I have chosen to call "covenant-breaking". This is a catch-all phrase to encapsulate all the sins and violations of vows in a marriage. A covenant may be defined as *"a sacred bond between a man and a woman instituted by and publicly entered into before God (whether or not this is acknowledged by the married couple) normally consummated by sexual intercourse."*[43]   A divorce is basically a breach of the marital covenant whereby one or both parties violated his or her *vows of faithfulness* to that sacred bond. The proponents of covenant marriage insist that it is not just a bilateral legal contract between the man and woman, but is also a sacred bond that includes God.

Sins of Unfaithfulness

We could summarize the previous biblical grounds for divorce under one heading: *unfaithfulness.* Sexual immorality would be *unfaithfulness* to the vows of sexual exclusiveness. Desertion could be defined as *unfaithfulness* in not providing the daily duties vowed to be a husband or wife. Abuse and neglect would be *unfaithfulness* in loving, cherishing and nourishing. In fact, just about any violation of the vows and promises, could be termed *unfaithfulness!* This paints the marriage duties with a broad brush!

The question is, "How do *you* define unfaithfulness?" Sexual unfaithfulness is defined from "some uncleanness" (Deut. 24:1) to "adultery" (Exodus 20:14). Adultery, however, has also been suggested to include more than just sexual "unfaithfulness". For example, adultery is used as a figure of speech when describing God "divorcing" Judah for her adulteries (See Ezekiel 23:9-33; Malachi 2:10-16). Likewise, when Ezra (Ezra 9-10) was commanded to supervise the divorces of hundreds of Israelite men who had married foreign women, it was because the pagan women had taught them to become idol worshippers. So, the term "unfaithfulness" or "adultery" has been used to mean spiritual infidelity as well as sexual infidelity. Both Judah and Israel broke faith with God by their spiritual infidelity. Their spiritual infidelity came about because they had married foreign wives who led them to worship other gods.

Thus, Shelly concludes, 'the repudiation of one's marital vows either by sexual infidelity or refusal to live in constant concern for one's mate constitutes adultery(i.e. covenant-breaking)"[44]. Adultery, according to this definition, may be defined as "unfaithfulness" whether it is sexual or otherwise. The Old Testament rabbis developed elaborate traditions to define when a husband might have grounds to divorce his wife because she "finds no favor in his eyes", including the frequency of sexual intercourse (Deut. 24:1). The vows of their covenant included "marital rights" (Exodus 21:10-11), but did not define "how frequent" the rights had to be exercised.

According to this position the specific sin appears to be a general breach of a sacred covenant. It really does not matter whether the breach was sexual infidelity or some other violation, the "breach of covenant" is the sin of which the offender must repent. Layfield agrees, "The issue is the *broken covenant*. The divorce sin is "breaking the covenant with a spouse or sending her away from him"[45]

Writers who take this position assume that the Bible speaks in general principles rather than specifics when stating allowable causes for divorce (Matthew 5:32; 19:9). Violations of the marital covenant may be according to the "letter" (sexual infidelity) or the "spirit" (pornography) of the law. The broken covenant position explains that pornography, physical abuse, chronic drug addictions, mental illness, imprisonment, and even laziness *might* become acceptable grounds for divorce in some cases. What this means according to Keener is: "Assuming that Jesus' teaching on the subject is a general principle meant to admit exceptions (as Matthew and Paul demonstrate), and acknowledging the probability that his teaching is hyperbolic, we may allow some exceptions not addressed by Matthew or Paul because they were not specifically relevant to the situations these writers addressed."[46]

Generally, the Old Testament rabbis agreed that valid grounds for divorce were childlessness, material neglect, emotional neglect, and sexual infidelity.[47] These four "causes" some believe, outlined the "any matter" list of the Pharisees in the debates with Jesus in the gospels. As they did with almost every other law of God, the "traditions of the rabbis" enlarged, defined, and added their traditions to the basic commands. "Unfaithfulness" was understood broadly as sexual immorality and was defined to also include the typical sexual violations such as illicit intercourse, adultery, incest, and homosexuality. In addition, the Jewish scribes, particularly the Pharisees, developed several tradition-defined forms of adultery. For example, "suspected adultery" could be charged from even a faint rumor or even if a woman was left alone with a man in a room. "Encouraging adultery" might be as simple as a woman going out of the house with her hair loose or her arms bare.

THE PAULINE PRIVILEGE

The teachings of the Apostle Paul in general, and the "Pauline Privilege" in particular, are important. We have already introduced you to issues of "spiritually incompatible" (believer/unbeliever) marriages and divorce. A more thorough study of 1st Corinthians 7 will help pull it all together. Paul wrote this chapter to answer questions asked by Christians in the church in Corinth (7:1) about marital issues. They were concerned about marriage in general, living single, spiritually mixed marriages, the marriages of widows and the marriages of virgins, and remarriage. The apostle also mentions the *circumstantial considerations* of "times of distress" (7:25-26).

READ 1st Corinthians 7:1-9

First, Paul argues that the state of being married is typically *better* than to live your life as a single. Why? Because of the sin of immorality. Not only that, but the marital state is one of God's prime relationships for training to do His work.

115

In fact, the sexual interaction of a husband and wife is very important in defeating Satan.

READ 1ˢᵗ Corinthians 7:10-16

Second, the Apostle Paul presents the grand ideal principle given by the Lord which plainly states: DO NOT DIVORCE! Divorce *should not* even be a topic of discussion for two believers in Christ! He says,

> *10 Now to the married I command, yet not I but the Lord: A wife is not to depart from her husband. 11 But even if she does depart, let her remain unmarried or be reconciled to her husband. And a husband is not to divorce his wife* (Compare Mark 10:5-9).

Then, he advises continuing spiritually mixed marriages between believers and unbelievers.

> *12 But to the rest I, not the Lord, say: If any brother has a wife who does not believe, and she is willing to live with him, let him not divorce her. 13 And a woman who has a husband who does not believe, if he is willing to live with her, let her not divorce him. 14 For the unbelieving husband is sanctified by the wife, and the unbelieving wife is sanctified by the husband; otherwise your children would be unclean, but now they are holy. 15 But if the unbeliever departs, let him depart; a brother or a sister is not under bondage in such cases. But God has called us to peace. 16 For how do you know, O wife, whether you will save your husband? Or how do you know, O husband, whether you will save your wife?*

As you read 1 Corinthians 7, you will see that we should use common sense and allow for circumstances in matters of divorce. A study of this passage, in conjunction with the others we have studied will help you form your own conclusions about biblical marriage and divorce.

Decisions in specific cases can be difficult. For example, how would you advise on the following marital situations? Could these individuals divorce with God's permission!?

- A husband (or wife) has a mate who verbally assaults him daily, to the point that he has contemplated suicide to escape the marriage.
- A husband (or wife) physically abuses his mate and the children on a regular basis. Members of the family, including the children, are threatened with death if they leave the abuser.
- A husband (or wife) regularly engages in pornography, and places sexual expectations on the mate that are difficult or conscientiously impossible to morally perform.
- A husband (or wife) is imprisoned for life due to crimes he has committed. Is remaining married to this person the only option open to the mate?

You decide! If you were in one of these situations, would you have acceptable Biblical grounds for divorce? If not, what options would be acceptable in a biblical marriage? Similar battlegrounds over *what's right* and *what's wrong* are confusing to many Biblical scholars and practicing ministers. The Apostle Paul does not give specific answers to the Corinthians to every conflicted issue, but he does give some principles and guidelines for them to make judgment calls. In summarizing this passage, Shelly concludes that *"Paul does not try to give a set of inflexible rules for solving complex dilemmas in human relationships. He appeals to each believer's desire to honor Christ in a culture that is often hostile to faith"*.[48] Situations like the ones noted above generate spiritual hostility and can destroy a marriage. Such marriages usually end in divorce ...or, even worse! Yes, there may be worse endings to a marriage than divorce – murder, suicide, loss of children, and estrangement from church and family!

When Jesus debated the Jewish leaders on the "Mosaic Toleration" of the Old Testament (Deuteronomy 24:1-4), he gave the core principle for biblical marriage, *don't divorce*! Paul, on the other hand, addressed believers, both Jews and Gentiles many of the gentiles who had recently come out of morally decadent paganism, in which worship involved temple prostitution and sexual orgies. Some of the Corinthian Christians were undoubtedly married to mates who continued to be such practicing pagans.

The city of Corinth was known far and wide as a center of sexual indulgence and other forms of immorality. From this background two groups existed in the Corinthian church regarding sexual activities. First, there were those who had come directly from the Greco/Roman influence of permissive, immoral sexual relations. (See 1 Corinthians 6:12-20). The second group forbade all sexual relations, including those in a valid marriage. (See 1 Corinthians 7:1-2). It wasn't just a reaction. There were many Greek proponents of celibacy because of Pythagomas and Aristotles' influence. That's where the early Christian error came from too.

This passage prompts us to consider the background, the cultural conditions, and the context of marriage. Paul wrote to a very diverse group of Christians to answer their questions about marriage,. Let us summarize Paul's writings in 1st Corinthians 7 for those who were married, unmarried, virgins, and widows.

First, Paul taught that we should respect the principle of being married over living single (1st Corinthians 7:2-5).

Marriage is right and honorable as an institution ordained by God. Paul confirmed the principles that began when man and woman were first brought together in marriage. The formula for a marriage is simple: *a man having his own wife and a wife having her own husband.* Monogamy is not only confirmed by this formula, but implied to be God's plan for life. Respecting marriage includes respect for the *boundaries of marriage to control sexual immorality* by providing a socially and spiritually valid platform for sexual intercourse and the legitimacy of children (See 7:14). *Sexual relations are valid and right in marriage,* therefore each partner has a responsibility to not "deprive" his/her mate of sexual interaction (vs.5). If a person chooses to be *unmarried or is a widow, he or she must be willing and able to control* his or her passion for sexual relations; otherwise, these individuals should marry.

Second, believers married to believers should keep their marriage vows and not divorce. (1 Corinthians 7:10-11)

The permanence of marriage was commanded by Jesus as the divine plan from creation. (See Mark 10:11-12; Luke 16:18). Believers should strive to maintain their marriages and not divorce. Divorce (departing, separating) is a possibility for believers, but they should strive to maintain their marriages. Here Paul affirms for the first time that a woman might initiate the divorce (departing) in accordance with the contemporary Roman law for divorce. If believers do divorce they should allow ample time after separation for the possibility of reconciliation.

Third, believers married to unbelievers should keep their marriage vows and (if possible) not divorce. (1 Corinthians 7:12-16)

There is a higher probability of divorce in a mixed marriage with spiritual incompatibility than in a marriage of two believers who are spiritually compatible. Believers who find themselves in marital covenants with spiritually incompatible mates should make every effort to make the marriage work for many reasons, including the following: a). Marriage "sanctifies" (sets apart) the children (possibly, for

God).   The Christian influence on rearing children is affirmed, b). The believer may save (convert) the unbeliever to become a believer.   Properly performed duties in a marriage can be strong motivators for individuals to change. (See 1 Peter 3:1-4). In addition, believers should seek peace in a marriage as in other aspects of their lives. Even in mixed marriages, believers are to honor their marriage vows. But, if the unbeliever "departs" (divorces) the believer is not "under bondage".

Fourth, Christians should (try to) remain in the state of marriage in which they are called.

This general principle throughout the chapter can to be summarized by comparing several translations of verse 20:

Let each one remain in the same calling in which he was called. (NKJV)

Everyone should stay in the calling in which he was called (NIV)

So don't try to change what you were when God chose you. (Contemporary English Version)

Each person should stay the way he was when God called him (Easy-to-Read Translation)

Consider your own situation, re-living your divorce has been painful! It is both troubling and possibly confusing to attempt to understand the mind of God on this matter. However, your basic task has been: TO CONFIRM YOUR FAITH IN GOD AND HIS WORD!

We have summarized four general arguments on grounds for divorce that, according to some scholars, that would be acceptable to God. You have read and studied many of the

Biblical passages they use to establish their views. Divorce is an ugly and complicated question, even for the scholars!

I hope that one thing is clear from the past two chapters! Christians who sincerely seek after God's plan for Biblical marriage will _strive_ to maintain their marriages so long as possible while considering divorce only as a very last resort.

Chapter 7

FORGIVENESS:

TO SIN IS HUMAN, TO FORGIVE IS DIVINE!

Seeker's Task #7: Seek and Give *forgiveness* for past sins.

> *Just when you think the hard part is over, God gives you another*
> *mountain to climb in your quest for biblical marriage! As a*
> single, *again you have gone through, or currently have, feelings of*
> *anger, abandonment, rejection, resentment, bitterness, and possibly*
> *even hate! Your task now is to seek and to give forgiveness. You*
> *will not be able to move on until you spiritually experience*
> *forgiveness based on God's Word. The task of this segment of your*
> *journey is to achieve human forgiveness.   Reviewing God's*
> *forgiveness will come later!*

I had been randomly called as a volunteer chaplain to
"come visit a young woman who was in deep depression".

Tina was a frail 28-year old mother of two. She was in the psychiatric ward at the hospital after attempting to take her own life. When I first saw her, she had matted hair and tear-drenched red cheeks. She was sitting on the side of the bed, rocking back and forth, and mumbling over and over again, *"I'm just no good. I'm just dirty. I feel so dirty…so dirty…I'm no good… dirty…"*

Hearing that I was a minister, she began to pour out her story to this young "priest". Tina had become sexually involved with a man in the same apartment building where she lived. Her husband, a young up-and-coming businessman, rushed her to the hospital when he found her unconscious, but he knew nothing of why she wanted to end her life! What was she going to do?

That incident happened more than fifty years ago, but I have thought about Tina a lot through the years. I only saw her that one time, but I have wondered what happened to her. Did she tell her husband that she had been sexually immoral? Did he forgive her? Did she ever forgive herself? Did her marriage survive, or did it end in divorce? What happened to her two children? Was she successful later in taking her own life? I just don't know.

What I do know is that Tina was burdened down with pain because of her sins of unfaithfulness. She had been sexually immoral and knew she had hurt a lot of people. She had betrayed her husband and her children. She had gambled her entire life for one fleeting hour of lust and sex. Her guilt was literally eating her alive! She expressed feelings of hopelessness, shame and fear and of being all alone! Most of all as a wayward Catholic, she felt God was far away! Tina was emotionally paralyzed by her guilt. For her, life seemed to be over. She thought, "There is *nothing* for me in the future!"

Jim Smoke said, "one of the greatest therapies that God ever gave to man was the therapy of forgiveness."[49] He lists six things to consider when forgiving yourself:

- I accept my humanity as a human being
- I have the freedom to fail.
- I accept responsibility for my failures.
- I can forgive myself for my failures.
- I accept God's forgiveness.
- I can begin again.

Tina was struggling with how to find the path to forgiveness. She felt that her husband would never forgive her, and neither could she forgive herself. And, more importantly, she did not see how God could forgive her. Her road to living was defined by her ability to accept forgiveness.

FORGIVENESS: THE KEY TO MOVING ON

Forgiveness is the key to your spiritual recovery, the restoration of your faith and how successfully you move on! Forgiveness is very important in your journey. Forgiveness is how you settle the issues of rejection and abandonment, anger and bitterness, and all the other sins that have burdened your heart and impeded your life. Your experiences may not have been the same as those of Tina, but you probably have many of the same feelings of despair and worthlessness. Like Tina you may be caught in the trap of unforgiveness! Do you wonder what is just "over the next hill" for you? Do you know it is time to "move on", but you wonder *how?* The answer is found in one word: FORGIVENESS! Forgiveness has a life-giving power! It is the way you manage your wrongs with others. It is the door to your daily approach to God. Unforgiveness is a death-producing cancer that eats at you daily!

Forgiveness! *For What?*

First, you should look back to where you have been in your quest for pleasing God. Your spiritual journey in seeking *biblical marriage* has taken you from the blossoming of desire in youth as a single, through the idyllic halls of biblical marriage, and out the door of divorce or death! Your tour has brought up old memories of painful (even sinful!) actions. You have had to make some personal decisions about "What *really* happened? You have read from the Word of God so that you can *know* His will on the matter, and reviewed conventional wisdom and scholarly commentaries on these same issues.

Now, you want to "move on" with your life! But before we go there, remind yourself of the clear maxims you have discovered along the way:

1) *Pleasing God should be your number one goal in life!* We, *both* men and women, are created in His image. You represent Him on earth to do His work. *Faithfulness to God* must be your number one priority! Regardless of what happened in your marriage or what sins might have destroyed it, being faithful to God *now* (pleasing Him!) *trumps* everything else.

2) *Being Single (a virgin) or Single, again, widowed (by death of spouse) or unmarried (divorced), can be the best of times and the worst of times at the same time!* Living single may be desirable *if* you have the gift from God to maintain your sexual purity. If living single is your choice you must observe voluntary celibacy, because sexual relations are only morally acceptable inside the state of marriage. This reality is the controlling rule for virgins, widows, and others who are unmarried (divorced). Otherwise the scriptures say, "let them marry" (1 Corinthians 7:2, 9, 28, 36, 39).

3) *Biblical marriage is still God's best plan for a man or a woman to learn the important godly practices of faithfulness, love, trust, commitment, obedience and forgiveness.* These God-like traits are essential in representing His image to a lost world. Biblical marriage is the platform where a husband and a wife learn obedience (submission) by complementing each other as intimate mates. Husbands learn to take *the lead.* Wives learn to be *submissive* as suitable helpers. Both are to *faithfully* serve God. In addition, Biblical marriage is the protected place where the intimacy of sexual interaction *creates* new life!

4) *Those who are married should strive to remain faithfully married and should not divorce.* Although there may be circumstances where this is not possible, the basic rule for Christians is, *if possible maintain your marriage.* Divorce itself is sinful under some circumstances. Either the act of divorce, or the fact that one or both partners commit sins that bring it about, makes all divorce sinful in one respect. In Chapter six we discussed allowable grounds for divorce in detail.

5) *Sin plays a leading role in destroying any marriage. Sins always demand forgiveness!* In one way or another, sinful behaviors are probably at the heart of every marriage that ends in divorce. Sexual unfaithfulness, perhaps the most serious of sins, is probably the most *uncommon* reason to divorce. The more common sins that bring about divorce are such things as sinful anger, malice and bitterness, lying and slander, jealousy, hate, breach of vows by emotional, physical and verbal abuse and other violations of the marital covenants. These sins can only be resolved by forgiveness.

Forgiving Yourself, and Others

Forgiveness is the process of ending *resentment*, *indignation* *or* *anger as a result of perceived offenses, differences or mistakes, and the ceasing to demand punishment or restitution.* Effective forgiveness is a two-part process: 1). emotional release from negative feelings, and 2). relinquishing the rights of punishment.

Forgiveness gives you the ability to let go of the past. Presently we are focusing on your forgiveness on a human level, not your forgiveness from God! However, the forgiveness you seek from God is also critically important and will be the focus of your journey in the next chapter. Your quest now in learning *how* forgiveness works will later help you *know* God's forgiveness for you. Forgiveness is giving up your right to hurt others because they hurt you! Forgiveness "101" is nothing more than a clear decision to just *let go* of the past!

THE POISON OF AN UNFORGIVING HEART

The key to successfully living in the single, *again* state is learning *how to give and accept forgiveness.* You cannot continue to live in anger, bitterness or guilt! Some sage has said, *"Not forgiving is the poison we drink, hoping someone else will die!"* Your forgiveness will take on three forms: 1). Forgiving others who have sinned against you, 2). Accepting forgiveness from others against whom you have sinned, and 3). Forgive yourself.

READ Hebrews 12:12-15 (We will call you back to this chapter many times!)

12 Therefore strengthen the hands which hang down, and the feeble knees, 13 and make straight paths for your feet, so that what is lame may not be dislocated, but rather be healed. 14 Pursue peace with all people, and holiness, without which no one will see the Lord: 15 looking carefully lest anyone fall short of the grace of God; lest any root of bitterness springing up cause trouble, and by this many become defiled

Another expression for "root of bitterness" is "hard feelings". Your feelings are hard because you have allowed angry thoughts to fester over time. You have re-played your hurts, failures, and sins over and over in your mind! The pain you felt has calcified your feelings and hardened your resolve to *force* accountability in others! When you have hard feelings, you can be sure it is your unforgiving heart that has created the calluses.

There are several reasons why forgiveness is so important. First and foremost, *"if (you) forgive men their trespasses, your heavenly Father will also forgive you: But if you forgive not men their trespasses, neither will your heavenly Father forgive your trespasses."*(Matthew 6:14-15). Finding your forgiveness from God depends on your ability to forgive others. In addition, the *perfect peace* of mind we all crave comes from your understanding of forgiveness. Peace and forgiveness are firmly centered on the things of God (See Isaiah 26:3).

READ Matthew 18:21-35

In fact, forgiving others is something Jesus said we must *do over* and *over* and *over again*! (Matthew 18:21-22). In this context, Peter asked the question: "How often (many times!)...shall I forgive...?" Jesus answered, "Seventy times seven", or literally 490 times! WOW! Forgiveness, Jesus implied, *is literally* at the heart of true religion.

To illustrate this point Jesus told the story of a certain king who wanted to settle accounts with his servants. One could not pay, and the king forgave him the debt. The servant who had been forgiven his debt by the king then went out and found one of his fellow servants who owed him a debt. He refused to forgive him even though that servant fell down at his feet and begged him for mercy! Word got back to the king that the forgiven servant would not extend forgiveness to another servant. The king was angry, called the servant in and said, *"You wicked servant! I forgave you…should you not also forgive your fellow servant…?* The passage concludes with this simple statement: *"So My heavenly Father also will do to you if each of you, from his heart, does not forgive his brother his trespasses."* (18:35). James adds that *"judgment is without mercy to one who has shown no mercy. Mercy triumphs over judgment"* (James 2:13)! The Biblical meaning of "mercy" is to be spared or rescued from judgment, harm, danger, or trouble. True forgiveness has mercy imbedded in it!

You just can't keep score while you forgive! Forgiveness should flow *continually* from you to others and from others to you. Another way you can understand the powerful force of forgiveness is to review the forgiveness God offers us when we sin.

Forgiveness is always the only good answer to sin, but forgiving is a hard thing to *do*. We often mistakenly think that forgiveness means that we should say, "All is forgiven and forgotten and things will go back to what they were!" That usually does not happen. Our forgiveness of others may require nothing more than just a decision to forgive. We don't have to condone what's been done. What *was* wrong is *still* wrong! We don't have to invite the person back into our lives or even to be friendly with them. However, our forgiving others must be modeled after the forgiveness extended to us by God.

You must allow yourself to release all the negative emotions associated with the person who hurt you! As long as you hold onto the pain, you are *choosing* to allow that person's past actions to continue to hurt you. You can *choose* to stop letting them hurt you by refusing to have the negative thoughts of unforgiveness. That's a definition of forgiveness that's doable for those of us who are less than God. To *forgive* is a decision *you* make! Those you are forgiving may or may not accept your forgiveness. That makes it more difficult, but not impossible. Remember, God's forgiveness is what you are seeking. It will help you to know more about how God forgives.

GOD'S FORGIVENESS

All sins grieve God, whether they are committed against a former spouse or others!

> *"Then the LORD saw that the wickedness of man was great in the earth, and that every intent of the thoughts of his heart was only evil continually. And the LORD was sorry that He had made man on the earth, and <u>He was grieved in His heart</u>."* (Genesis 6:5-6).

1). God's Forgiveness is Merciful but has Consequences

Mercy is a powerful, deep awareness of someone else's suffering when you want them <u>not</u> to suffer. Mercy means the giving of grace to people *who don't deserve it* or showing compassion to someone over whom you have power or authority. Mercy is the effect of grace on justice. It is rooted in <u>love</u>: *God shows mercy because God loves us and forgives us.*

Paul, the "chief of sinners" explains the meaning of a proper merciful attitude:

READ: 1ˢᵗ Timothy 1:12-17

And I thank Christ Jesus our Lord who has enabled me, because He counted me faithful, putting me into the ministry, 13 although I was formerly a blasphemer, a persecutor, and an insolent man; but I obtained mercy because I did it ignorantly in unbelief. 14 And the grace of our Lord was exceedingly abundant, with faith and love which are in Christ Jesus. 15 This is a faithful saying and worthy of all acceptance, that Christ Jesus came into the world to save sinners, of whom I am chief.

16 However, for this reason I obtained mercy, that in me first Jesus Christ might show all longsuffering, as a pattern to those who are going to believe on Him for everlasting life. 17 Now to the King eternal, immortal, invisible, to God who alone is wise, be honor and glory forever and ever. Amen.

Our God is a longsuffering, forgiving God! He is both "righteous" (just) and "merciful" (compassionate) in how he treats those who sin against him. (See Romans 5:8)

But, God's forgiveness is *not without consequences*. Sins are damaging to everything that comes in contact with them! In the case of David's adultery with Bathsheba (2 Samuel 11-12) other damaging sins were also involved, including lying and murder. Many people were hurt. One consequence of the sin which could not be reversed was that Uriah lost his life!

David repented of his sin (2 Samuel 11:13), but he never forgot it (Psalms 51:3)! His enemies *continued* to "whisper together against him" and his friends turned against him when he stumbled (Psalms 41:4-9). In addition, the child that was born from the adulterous sin died (2 Samuel 11:15-19) and David's whole family suffered from hatred and murder. Nathan's sermon to David was concise and clear . What he had done would change things, even though David (and probably Bathsheba) sought and received forgiveness. "Repentance does not enable someone to 'unscramble eggs" (i.e., undo harm already done, put back together a shattered relationship) but accepts responsibility, confesses sin, accepts forgiveness, and pledges to seek God's help never to commit the same transgression in the future"[50]

Mercy and forgiveness are critically important for both those who sin, and for those who have been sinned against! God can forgive our sins. But, even with forgiveness, consequences of marriage sins can reverberate into the future. Others suffer. Many lives are changed because your marriage

ended in divorce. David Instone-Brewer concludes his
research on "Divorce and Remarriage in the Church" by
noting that it "demonstrates God's continuing love for us,
even after the sin of breaking marriage vows..."[51]

> *The LORD is slow to anger and abundant in lovingkindness,
> forgiving iniquity and transgression; <u>but He will by no means clear
> {the guilty,}</u> visiting the iniquity of the fathers on the children to
> the third and the fourth generations* (Numbers 14:18).

2). *God's Forgiveness is Conditional but not Condemning*

READ John 8:1-11

Jesus was tested concerning his attitude toward one who
was "caught in the very act" of adultery. There is no better
place to begin than here to see God's attitude toward the
sinner in such a marital meltdown. .. *and* to see his work of
forgiveness! The concluding verses in this passage are a
tremendous resource for such sinners:

> *"Jesus looked up and said to her, "Woman, where are they? Has
> no one condemned you?" She said, "No one, Lord." And Jesus
> said, "Neither do I condemn you; go, and do not sin again."*
> (John 8:10-11)

Your sins in a former marriage may be branded upon
your heart! You can give vivid details of the battles you
fought and the guilt of sin that has ensued. Many divorcees
continue to harbor the memories, display the scars, and feel
the guilt from marriages that ended years ago! Two truths of
Biblical forgiveness are reflected in this text:

1) God forgives even the worst sins! ("caught in the act
   of adultery")
2) We must repent, stop sinning ("go, sin no more")

The Apostle John adds a third truth in his first epistle

3) We must confess our sins to God.

If we say that we have no sin, we deceive ourselves, and the truth is not in us. 9 If we confess our sins, He is faithful and just to forgive us our sins and to cleanse us from all unrighteousness. 10 If we say that we have not sinned, we make Him a liar, and His word is not in us. : (1 John 1:9).

God's forgiveness means that He accepts you as a person, but you may experience other consequences because of the sins you have committed.

3). God's Forgiveness is Full and Complete!

Full forgiveness from God follows a sinner's commitment to stop sinning (repentance) *and* a confession, acknowledgment of wrong! John indicates that based on these conditions the goodness, justice, and faithfulness of God will *"cleanse us from all unrighteousness (sin)"* God fully forgives *and forgets* our sins!

"I, even I, am he who blots out your transgressions, for my own sake, and remembers your sins no more" (Isaiah 43:25).

It is possible for the Lord to look at you *without seeing your past sins* because when He forgave you He removed your sins "as far as the east is from the west" (Psalm 103:12).   God's forgiveness is complete!

READ 1 Corinthians 6:9-11

The Apostle Paul defined the full impact and power of God's forgiveness on human sinfulness when he cataloged the marvelous changes in the lives of the Corinthians. They were sinful and lost prior to their conversions, but their relationship to God was changed by His forgiveness:

> *And such were some of you. But you were washed, but you were sanctified, but you were justified in the name of the Lord Jesus and by the Spirit of our God* (1 Corinthians 6:11).

4). God's Forgiveness Covers All Sins

All of us have sinned. (Romans 3:23) All sin is a transgression of God's law by "missing the mark", falling short, or flagrantly disobeying God. Our misdeeds, mistakes, and sinful conduct may result in different consequences for our lives, but the bottom line is the same: GOD FORGIVES ALL SINS! That is, all but *one!* The "unpardonable sin"!

There is *one sin that is unpardonable!* That is the sin against the Holy Spirit, or blasphemy against the Holy Spirit. (Matthew 12:22-32; Mark 3:22-27; Luke 11:17-23) That sin must have been a sin committed by those who, in the face of Jesus' divine powers, said he had an unclean spirit (demon)! Notice that Jesus does not mention anything about marital relationships when describing the unpardonable sin! Sins like fornication and adultery or some of the more common marital sins such as uncontrolled anger and slander; harsh verbal abuse; jealousy and malice; or the breaking of one's vows are not even mentioned in these passages!

READ Mark 3:28-30

"Assuredly, I say to you, all sins will be forgiven the sons of men, and whatever blasphemies they may utter; but he who blasphemes against the Holy Spirit never has forgiveness, but is subject to eternal condemnation"-- because they said, "He has an unclean spirit."

5). God's Forgiveness of Sin…includes Adultery!

READ: 1 Corinthians 6:9-11

Do you not know that the unrighteous will not inherit the kingdom of God? Do not be deceived. Neither fornicators, nor idolaters, nor adulterers, nor homosexuals, nor sodomites, nor thieves, nor covetous, nor drunkards, nor revilers, nor extortioners will inherit the kingdom of God. And such were some of you. But you were <u>washed</u>, but you were <u>sanctified</u>, but you were <u>justified</u> in the name of the Lord Jesus and by the Spirit of our God.

Here Paul makes a clear distinction between the unrighteous state of "fornicators, idolaters, adulterers, homosexuals, sodomites, thieves, covetous, drunkards, revilers, and extortioners" and those who had been "washed", "sanctified" and "justified"!   Obviously some of the Corinthian Christians formerly engaged in some of these sins. But they had been forgiven, saved from their sins!   They became Christians because *"many of the Corinthians hearing, believed and were baptized* (See 1 Corinthian 18:8). Thus, due to their "washing" in the blood of Christ and their being "justified and sanctified" by the gospel of Christ; they were no longer viewed by God as the sinners they were formerly! The forgiveness of God covers all sin, --completely and forever!

Forgive like God

God's forgiveness is the standard by which you should evaluate your own forgiveness of others!   We all understand that we fall short of the glory of God (Romans 3:23). Whatever ability and strength we have to forgive those who have hurt us deeply must come as a gift of God. We must pattern our forgiveness after God's. Because we are created in the image of God, we have a responsibility to be like Him and to properly represent Him in our lives.

Be merciful, forgive*!*

The compassion of heaven caused Jesus to weep over the city of Jerusalem (Matthew 23:37) but they would not change! Jesus did not want them to suffer, but the entire city was destroyed in 70 A. D. by Titus and the Roman armies. Having a forgiving spirit may not change the outcome, but it changes the heart of the one who has it.

Many divorcees endure years of hurt, sometimes also causing the hurt of others. Memories of their painful experiences plague their lives daily. Forgiveness is the only way to halt the continued pain of those memories. It is a rational decision that looks forward instead of backward.

Act responsibly, change*!*

The Apostle Paul models for us what happens after we forgive. We change! Repentance is godly sorrow for our participation in sinning against God. Paul wanted to serve God before his sinfulness of persecuting God's people. After his repentance and conversion as the chief of sinners he was even more committed to doing God's will.

The woman caught in the very act of adultery was given the formula for her future: "go and sin no more"! It is obvious that a person can change following forgiveness. After forgiveness a person focuses on being right with God more than ever before!

Remember No more!

Here is where the ideal standards of God are real challenges for the sinner! David remembered his sin and probably all the people he had hurt. Paul could look back and call himself the "number one sinner" because of the bad things he had done! This point has more to do with a person forgiving him/herself, rather than forgiving someone else.

There is some comfort in knowing that all of us are sinners! No one has a right to point a finger or cast a stone at anyone else. Sins may vary in their consequences, but in the eyes of God all sins fall into a single group: transgressions against God! Those who need to forgive themselves would do well *to forget*…at *least forget the need to retaliate against someone* (including yourself!) for the sins that have been committed. Stop hurting others, and stop feeling hurt!

Moving On…

Single, *again* emotions can range from feelings of confusion, self-doubt, anger, ambivalence and, in some cases sheer relief! Life as you knew it is over, and now you have the job of building a new life. This will take *time* and *work* as you find your niche in your new world.

Chapter 8

SPIRITUAL RECOVERY:

"TAKE THE NEXT RIGHT TURN"

Seeker's Task #8: Begin turning your life around!

> *Your life is very different now from your life just a few short months ago! We have described it in terms of "a personal loss", "a wreck" and "a death"! However, losing a life-partner cannot be adequately described by any of these analogies. How do you recover from such a loss? Where do you start in getting things back to what we call "normal"?*

The Chinese had a proverb for this task: "A journey of a thousand miles begins with the first step!" Your task at this point is to *begin* the recovery process...one step at a time!

Very simply, you are just *beginning* the long journey back! Let patience be your friend and don't give up.

Matt's marriage was troubled, but for the sake of his young boys he had made the commitment, in his words, "to work it out". He was a brilliant salesman who literally exuded confidence and personal power, yet his perceived invincibility opened him up to dangerous options, including substance abuse. He honestly admitted his faults and vowed to correct them. He was seeing a professional counselor. He really wanted to "do the right thing"! But he was in a troubled marriage, and his recovery must have looked like the tallest mountain in the world for him to climb! In our last telephone conversation before he succumbed to the pressures of his life, I asked him what he was going to do. "I am going to do the next right thing!" was his answer. The next right thing! One step can be the beginning of a "thousand mile journey",... or not! In Matt's case he just seemed to give up!

(These words are being penned on the third anniversary in August when our grandson made the decision to go home and be with the Lord! -grh)[52]

SPIRITUAL RECOVERY

If your marriage ended abruptly in divorce it probably had been battered by volleys of sin for a long time. You just feel sick about it! Sick of battling the lies and charades! Sick of trying to make it work! Sick to the soul because the most beautiful thing two people could ever have imagined somehow went very wrong! In such cases the death of the marriage does feel like a sickness, a spiritual sickness! Not only was your marriage terminated, the process also took away your sense of well-being! Terrible sins in your marriage such as abandonment, rejection, anger, malice, slander, abuse, and even sexual infidelity may still burden your memories and cloud your vision for the future. In many ways, you might have felt that your life was virtually over! Many do just give up.

If you are single, *again* because of the death of your mate, your situation is somewhat different. You do experience many of the same feelings that a divorcee has, but your recovery process may be different. The next chapter on faith and trust will probably be more helpful to you than the current one.

But, regardless, you are determined to recover and move on with your life. Recovery may be defined as: "the *return* to health from sickness; to *regain* something that has been lost; to *restore* what is damaged, or changed". These three words capture the structure of spiritual recovery: *return* to God, *regain* the relationships you lost, and *restore* a sense of spiritual well-being. Your goal is to become whole again . Your journey toward that goal ideally should include some sort of apology/acknowledgment that sins have been committed. Confessing and repenting of sin is critical to your recovery.

REPENTANCE: A RE-TURN TO GOD

"Losing a mate is a life-changing experience" understates the situation! No one can describe your loneliness and sense of abandonment...even from the presence of God! Your most important step in coming home is to return to God! Everything else will fall into place if you are in the right place with your Lord! This means turning from the *sins committed*. Repentance! Possibly, the most difficult thing you will do! Accepting forgiveness and extending forgiveness also are often difficult to do.

Sins *committed* are the driving force pushing repentance. For example, consider the ugly scarlet sin of sexual immorality. Jesus identified sexual immorality as grounds for allowable divorce when the Pharisees tested him on what the law taught . (Matt. 5:31-32; 19:8-9). Paul instructed the church in Corinth to withdraw fellowship from a member guilty of this sin. (1 Corinthians 5:1-5). But there are also other sins that require repentance.

The example of David and Bathsheba (2 Samuel 11-12) gives a graphic picture of why sexual immorality, not to mention lying and murder, are so *sinful*, especially regarding the consequences resulting from such sinful conduct. This story chronicles the secrecy, deceitfulness, and viciousness of sexual immorality and its far-reaching consequences. Bathsheba's marriage was destroyed. Her husband, Uriah, was murdered. David lied to his commanding officer. Others, including the commanding officer, became complicit in following David's sin with Bathsheba. The child that resulted from the sin died. The story has been repeated and passed on for numerous generations since.

Yet it is also the story of repentance and forgiveness. When David committed adultery, lied about the situation, misused his power as a commander, and was guilty of murder, he said that he sinned against "You and You only" – against God! Ideally in any divorce situation, you should consider some sort of apology/acknowledgment of sins. This is a difficult thing to do, but confession is a part of the recovery process. Confession to the "ex" or soon-to-be "ex" may not be possible, but confessing sins to God, and/or to the fellowship of your faith, the church, is essential!

The marital union that ensued between David and Bathsheba later produced the blood linage of Jesus. The very son of God was descended from these two sinful individuals. This fact alone should modify your ideas about God's forgiveness and the ability of God to make something good happen from something so ugly. It may be difficult for you to maintain such spiritual balance, to see yourself as a broken jar of clay yet with treasures of spiritual life and eternal worth inside. It's so much easier to think "I've been wronged" and to deny the presence of any guilt—or to say "I'm no good" or "I'm damaged goods," and pull away from God and His people, and seek a fallen place in a fallen world. Either of these extremes makes repair and restoration very hard if not impossible.

RE-READ John 8:1-11

Another example of sexual immorality is displayed in the case of this woman *caught in the very act* of sexual immorality! They thought the evidence was there. The witnesses seemed more than ready to cast the first stone as legal and biblical consequences for her sin. But, was that really true?

Jesus knew the duplicity of the Pharisees. He also understood the heart of the woman who had sinned. Jesus pointed toward repentance when he said to her, *"Neither do I condemn you, go and sin no more."* WOW! God does look on the heart! He and *He alone* can know if a person truly repents!

READ Ephesians 5:21-33

Failure to be a responsible husband or wife can also be a sin. This would include sins of omission by husbands or wives who did not perform God-mandated duties to their mates. Such sins violate the vows of the marriage pertaining to headship and submission roles, as well as mutual love and respect, including sexual fulfilment.

In addition to these, *any sin* that is chronically practiced can destroy a marriage. These might include such abusive practices as slander, gossip, backbiting, wickedness, covetousness, maliciousness, envy, murder, strife, evil-mindedness, violence, untrustworthiness, unloving, unforgiving, unmerciful, etc. (See Romans 1:24-32; Galatians 5:19-21). You may have been guilty of sins such as this in your previous marriage. Now is the time for you to turn from those things in genuine repentance.

What is Repentance?

The clearest example of repentance from sin in the New Testament may be found in the story of the prodigal son (Luke 15). The prodigal said, "I have sinned against heaven." (Luke 15:21) Then he did something about it. He said, *"I will arise... and he arose"* (Luke 15:18, 20). In the case of David's sin with Bathsheba, David confessed his sin to God-- *"For I will declare mine iniquity: I will be sorry for my sin."* (Psa. 38:18). In another Bible example the publican beat upon his breast, and said, *"God be merciful to me a sinner."* (Luke 18:13).

Repenting of wrongs is at the core of spiritual recovery. It begins with godly sorrow. It results in turning, changing! Practically speaking, "repent" simply means to change, to turn around! Take the next *right* turn! Turn from your old ways, including the sins of your previous marriage, and start over. This is the time for you to re-evaluate your goals, values, behaviors *and* relationships...then take a *turn in the right direction*! You are in the process of turning around! That process is *repentance*.

Repentance means to feel sorry, self-reproachful, or contrite for past conduct; regret or be conscience-stricken about a past action, attitude, etc. or, to feel such sorrow for sin or fault as to be disposed to change one's life for the better; be penitent. Repentance is a change of heart that results in a change of conduct. It begins with a mental decision that is prompted by godly sorrow. True repentance will result in changes in your life. Thus, a working definition of repentance is:

1) *To be sorry*: to recognize the wrong in something you have done and be sorry about it
2) *Then change*: to feel regret about a sin or past actions and change your ways or habits.

Basically, your repentance will be evident by changes in your personal life. These changes may also include new intimate relationships, a new support network, perhaps a new church family, possibly a move to a new location in a new home! Being single, *again* is always a transitional step to somewhere else. This is the time for you to "make some straight paths for your feet" (Hebrews 12:13). Things are going to change! *Plan well.*

Making Things Right

How do you take that next right turn?   More specifically, how do you make things right with God and others in your life? How do you repent of the sin, or sins, that have resulted in divorce. These questions usually are answered in regards to the rights for remarriage following a divorce.

J. D. Thomas, like many others, sees one spouse as the *innocent party in* some divorces and the other spouse is the *guilty party*[53] This designation is typically based on whether or not there were *allowable* grounds for divorce. One of the spouses was considered faithful to the terms of the biblical marriage and the other spouse violated the vows and committed a sin which would *allow* divorce. This position is most prevalent in the traditional views that either will not allow divorce for any cause, or for sexual immorality only. In some cases the *innocent party* may remarry, but the only two options for the *guilty party* are *reconciliation* or *the single life*[54] According to this view, the *only* ways to repent of the sin that caused the divorce are to either remain single for a lifetime, or return to the first spouse.

In reality, you may have committed multiple sins such as

8848

8888

8888

abuse, deprivation of sexual privileges or failure to nurture and cherish. The marriage may or may not include the sin of sexual immorality. Larry Richards considers the violations of the marital covenant allowable grounds[55] Craig Keener points to many of us when he says, "but when the case is genuinely too tough for us to judge, we ought to be humble enough not to judge it at all" [56] Rubel Shelly uses the term *"A Redemptive Theology"* to describe how divorced spouses and their sins should be resolved.[57] Regardless of the circumstances a loving God is always ready to forgive us of our sins if we repent.

All these writers believe that *divorce is bad, really bad!* The reason it is bad is because divorce usually involves sin. Those of us who want to be right with God know the need to confess our sins and repent of them. Ultimately all sins are against God, but your divorce might include sins against others. How do you correct them, and move on?

1) First, you go to God in the spirit of David (Psalms 38, 51) and confess your sins. Make your commitment to turn toward Him in faithfulness. Your first duty to yourself and to God is confession of sins.

2) Then you go to others who were hurt by your divorce, including your church, family and friends. If sins were involved, acknowledge such sins to those who suffered because of them. Change your will and decide to not continue sinning.

Turning back toward God is your first step in recovery but your task also includes making it "right" with others. Full recovery requires that you get back in the game, especially to perform your duties to God and others. This involves your attitudes and actions toward Him _and_ toward your friends and your family.

RESTORATION: REBUILDING RELATIONSHIPS

Jim Smoke notes a wise saying that applies to single, *again* recovery: "There are three things that make for happiness in living: something to do, someone to love, and something to look forward to." [58] Paul the Apostle described it like this:

> *...and reaching forward to those things which are ahead, I press toward the goal for the prize of the upward call of God in Christ Jesus. (Philippians 3:13-14).*

You will have to make things right with others if you truly want to make things right with God! During the process of your marriage ending, many of the closest and most cherished relationships of your life were also terminated. You may have burned your bridges in a futile attempt to light your way in your darkest hours. You thought you would *never* go back there again! But, now you miss those relationships.

READ 2 Corinthians 2:1-8

Many Christian brethren have become estranged due to very bizarre marital issues. In this passage a brother was guilty of flagrant sexual immorality, perhaps, even incest. But he repented. The Apostle Paul called the other brothers to forgive him lest the offender be overtaken by Satan in his sorrows. The instructions were clear: *"Therefore, I urge you to reaffirm your love to him." (2 Corinthians 2:8).*

READ 1 Corinthians 13:4-8

Re-building your burned bridges means that you first reaffirm your love for those of your lost relationships. Note how love behaves: "suffers long and is kind", "does not parade itself", "does not act rudely", "does not seek its own", "not easily provoked", "thinks no evil", "does not rejoice in iniquity", "believes…endures all things".

Now, apply these love-behaviors to your relationships with significant people in your past: former spouse, mother-in-law, family members, church family, friends, etc. In so far as it depends on you, live at peace with them. Your spiritual recovery is directly related to your willingness to reaffirm your love with these significant individuals and groups.

READ Romans 14:1-19

The storms of life have shaken everything you thought was on solid ground. Anxiety and worry have dominated you for a long time. You need the rest and peace that comes only through forgiveness and faith.

Re-connect by Faith

The biblical method for bridging any chasm that separates two people is simple: *Go…confess…forgive* (See Matthew 18:15-20; Romans 14:13-19). Re-building relationships is to "make peace" with yourself and others.

"Therefore, let us pursue the things which make for peace and the things by which one may edify another" (Romans 14:19).

READ Hebrews 12:1-14

The author of Hebrews (chapters 11-12) illustrated the power of faith by recounting a history of faith in action. Even though you might have burned your bridges to the past, your past is the core of who you are and the hope you have for the future. Faith forces you to "think back" and know that you are not alone! As much as possible, make things right with the people around you! "Lay aside" every "weight" (burden) from your past and get back into the race. The writer concludes by saying:

> *"Pursue peace with all men, and holiness, without which no one will see the Lord" (Hebrews 12:14).*

Finally, in rebuilding relationships, allow time for God in His providence to work. It takes time to heal hurt feelings and injured egos. Your task at this milestone is to *"begin"* turning your life around. You must make the commitment to do the next right thing to the best of your ability.

REJECTION OF GUILT AND SHAME

Our vocabulary often defines our theology when we speak of the "guilty party" and the "innocent party" in divorce. As we noted, some would argue that there is no "innocent" party in a divorce. Others support the belief that a biblical divorce may be caused by a guilty party against the will of an innocent party. My experience as a marital and family therapist is that guilt and shame always result following a divorce on the part of one, or both, of the parties.

Guilt is a direct result of sin, imagined or real. Guilt is the emotion we feel when we believe we have violated a moral or biblical standard by which we conduct our lives. The emotion is a human response based on the information received about questionable conduct of a husband or wife. Guilt is always about something we did, an act of behavior. It might stem from an innocent wife who decides to divorce (the act) a husband who is guilty of sexual immorality. Another spouse may experience pangs of guilt because of other sins committed in the marriage which are not simply defined in the divorce. It is not unusual for a widow or widower to feel guilty for whatever reason when the other spouse dies. "Why didn't I do more?", "I wish it had been me instead of her?" etc.

Guilt is usually a very debilitating emotion. It can lead to depression and even death. However, guilt can also be a constructive emotion to motivate you to do the right thing. In matters of sin, the conviction of guilt can lead to genuine repentance and change.

On the other hand, shame is usually destructive to human relationships. Remember, shame springs from guilt. Shame is not the same as guilt, but is related. Shame can be defined as "a painful emotion caused by consciousness of guilt, shortcoming, or impropriety". Others have distinguished between the two by indicating that we feel guilty for what we *do*, but we feel shame for what we *are*! Shame strikes at the core of our being, or own self-image of ourselves.

We know that doing the right thing is important to the Christian. But, it is very hard to know what the right thing *is* to do! Most Christians want to do their duties to God, but they are confused about what those duties are! In addition, when your duties become clearer, the weakness of the flesh challenges your performance. Paul said,

> *"For I have the desire to do what is right, but I cannot carry it out. For I don't do the good I want to do, but instead do the evil that I don't want to do."* (Romans 7:18-19)

The apostle Paul struggled with his desire to do right, and his ability to do it. If you want to do what's right, take the next right turn by taking this three-step process. This simple mental exercise works in helping you make the difficult decisions of life.

1) *Determine what is right in the eyes of God.*

This knowledge can only come from a basic study of God's Word and prayer (2 Timothy 3:14-17). Use the scriptures noted previously to determine *God's will* on the matter of biblical marriage. You will have a lot of different voices calling for you to remain faithful to God by going back to a former mate, or by remaining with your current mate, or by staying with your current mate but refraining from sexual relations. Others will say that the most acceptable spiritual relationship is for you to be single, celibate for the remainder of your life. There is wisdom in a multitude of counselors, but the only voice that really matters is the voice of God. Read His word. Study it! Pray to Him that your understanding may be enlightened (Ephesians 1:15-23). Listen to *His* counsel. You are your own priest! Study, let God speak to you through His Word.

But you must continue in the things which you have learned and been assured of, knowing from whom you have learned them, and that from childhood you have known the Holy Scriptures, which are able to make you wise for salvation through faith which is in Christ Jesus. All Scripture is given by inspiration of God, and is profitable for doctrine, for reproof, for correction, for instruction in righteousness, that the man of God may be complete, thoroughly equipped for every good work. (2 Timothy 3:14 -17)

2) *Decide to Do the right thing regardless of the consequences.*

Sin has consequences. Even though you may get forgiveness from your sins, the consequences may continue for generations to come. (See 2 Samuel 11:1-12:12). Make the *right thing* your priority and trust God to help you do it knowing that you may have to live with the consequences of your divorce. There will be many "unknowns" in the process, but the following step will help you with your decision.

3) <u>*Trust God!*</u>

Throughout this quest your number one priority has been your faithfulness to God! Whatever you do in anything, including marriage, your goal must be to obey God! Our love for God and our trust in God will calm our anxieties.

> *Therefore do not worry, saying, 'What shall we eat?' or 'What shall we drink?' or 'What shall we wear?' For after all these things the Gentiles seek. For your heavenly Father knows that you need all these things. But seek first the kingdom of God and His righteousness, and all these things shall be added to you. Therefore do not worry about tomorrow, for tomorrow will worry about its own things. Sufficient for the day is its own trouble.* (Matthew 6:31-34).

In the din of the noise from biblical scholars and other well-intentioned advisers, let God's voice guide your conscience. Listen to Him!

Recovery is a journey that begins with godly sorrow and turning toward God resulting in genuine repentance. But to be a successful journey, those single, *again* must get back in the game by resuming basic responsibilities to God and others. Your recovery will hinge on your ability to restore faithfulness to your life. Your contributions to those around you and to yourself are the faithful use of your time and talents. It's time for you to recover and resume your rightful place in your new world!

My friend Byron Brown paraphrased a passage from <u>Mere Christianity</u> by C. S. Lewis who fought in World War I and was wounded, carrying the bullet in him all of his life. Brown said, "I think it was, that in war, sometimes the safest thing to do is to leave the safety of the foxhole and change your position. Staying where you are feels safer for a moment, but in time it will place you in mortal danger. The longer you stay in it, the greater the danger grows. It must be a lot easier to stay in the "foxhole" of denial (and run the risk of committing the same sins again) or in the "foxhole" of "damaged goods" or depression and just float in the world—but the longer one stays there, the harder is it to get out alive".[59]

My goal in writing this chapter is to help you get out of the foxhole alive!

Chapter 9

RESTORING FAITHFULNESS:

ACCEPTING THE "NEW NORMAL"

Seeker's Task #9: Take your place in a Brave New World!!

> *Single, again, you are still in the game but your confidence has been severely challenged. You must pro-actively find and take your rightful position in God's world. Faith in yourself and in others will predict your future as you go forward.*

Matt was a delight to watch playing basketball. He was usually the smallest man on the court, but at point guard he was big! His quick hands and perceptive eyes gave us all a thrill when he would steal the ball or shoot a three-pointer. Most of the time he got it right, yet one of my enduring memories of Matt is seeing him hold his hand over his heart after making a mistake, look over at his coach, or the team, and mouth the words "My bad!" He was a team-player on a team which included the other players, the coaches, and even those of us in the stands. When he failed he felt like he owed us all an apology!

It is hard to perform at your peak when you think you are a failure. The loss of a marital partner is very different from failing to perform in a basketball game! However, those single, *again* experience many of the same challenges in life. In both cases there is a sense of failure, of not being faithful to the team. Failure tends to paralyze us, and we want to take ourselves out of the game at a time when we are really needed by the team! Marriage is truly a team experience.

The big difference between a basketball game and a failed marriage is the size of the loss that is experienced. David and Lisa Frisbie describe it like this: "Divorce is the death of together, the seemingly permanent end of forever ... Every morning of the twenty-first century many of us rise to face a new day without a partner. Someone promised us, "I do," but then didn't! Someone bravely said, "I will" –but when the times got tough, they wouldn't. Now we are alone, feeling branded with a daily sense of failure that shows itself in all we do".[60]

Biblical marriage as a team activity is also a covenant of faith, ---not just a legal contract. Actually, it is not just one covenant, but a whole bundle of agreements. "Covenant" is the catchword describing *"agreements you made to someone to do or not do something specific"*. In marriage the details of those agreements were generalized in the vows you took at the altar. Our vows are verbal statements of our word, but more than that, they define who we are, our core character! We sometimes urge couples to "keep your vows", when actually our marriage vows keep us! These public statements stand as guards over our relationships to remind us of our agreements (covenants!) and to protect us from failure. Vows, and the core character values they represent, are woven into the very fabric of our society in the form of legal laws and religious tenets. They stand as signposts to remind us of who we are and what we stand for, legally, ethically and religiously! Marriage vows lace together our past lives as individuals, our most intimate experiences with each other, and they even bind us to future generations. Violating *any* vow is serious stuff! Such a failure rips at the very fabric of our world.

READ Ecclesiastes 5:1-5, and Deuteronomy 23:21

Marriage is not *just* an experience of two individuals, but an experience that includes their extended families, their friends, ---yes, even *their entire community!* They are all bound together by agreements, written or unwritten. These covenants are defined by vows and taken as a whole they "embrace the sacredness of their (our) history together".[61]

Obviously, you and your chosen mate were covenant participants, but the list of fellow-travelers on your journey is much longer than just the two of you! It includes your immediate family members, your church-family brothers and sisters, and even stand-in friends. You made an agreement with each of these individuals in the spiritual history of your marriage; howbeit, a *very different* agreement from your marital vows with your mate!

The end of your marriage is proof-positive that covenants have been breached! Every participant who has a covenant-of-faith-interest in the marriage is affected. Each one will rally around to protect his or her covenant interests when the marriage is threatened, or ends. Emotions often flair and angry words pollute the air. Sometimes advice and counsel will be offered. Fault-finding and criticism are nearly always in abundance. However, little can be accomplished at this point by trying to establish blame. The useful purposes for guilt and shame in bringing about repentance have already been explored.

Your task now is to move on to a "new normal"! How you interact with this company of fellow-travelers is crucial to your new life in your new world.

PERSEVERANCE: A SPIRITUAL DISCIPLINE

Sure, you are discouraged and lonely and sad! After what you have gone through, who would not want to just give up! Losing a mate is painful and emotionally draining of every bit of optimism a person possesses! But, your life is *certainly* not over!

First, you must learn to just "keep on keeping on!" Don't take yourself out of the game! Maintain that which is *not* lost! This new relationship with friends and families _and_ your former spouse is much like that between God and His people. You are not the first to experience the pain of marital dissolution. The story of God and his people in the Old Testament is a history of a failed marriage. God hates divorce (Malachi 2:16) but he tolerated it (Deuteronomy 24). His relationship with his chosen people, often characterized as a marriage, resulted in divorce. In fact, throughout their tumultuous history God's "wife" was often unfaithful, but God kept taking her back. The truth of this Old Testament reference is about the faithfulness of God and how it compares with the unpredictable actions of his people. God is always steady, His people tend to be changeable. God's response, attitudes of heart and characteristics of actions demonstrated his faithfulness. This is the character trait we should practice, not the ugliness of the Old Testament people.

READ Hosea 1:2-5

Imagine it! God told His prophet to take a *harlot* to be his wife! Gomer's life was a history of unfaithfulness. As a harlot she was marked by her sexual immorality. But, God (working through Hosea) took her (Israel) for "his wife"! Perhaps she would change? NOT! The marriage was *continually* threatened by her sexual promiscuity. More than once...God's "wife", Israel, was unfaithful! But He maintained His faith in her! God treated her right even when she rejected Him.

READ Hosea 3:1-5

Hosea (God) took Gomer (Israel) back again and again! In fact, in this passage Hosea had to pay a price to get her back. Why? It would appear to most of us that Hosea (God) would have every right to say "No more! I am done with my wife (Israel)!" Why did he keep taking her back? The answer to this question comes in the following Scripture.

Read Hosea 6:1-6

The reason was that God wanted His wife (Israel) to return to Him! God wanted her to be saved. But when she returned He *expected* her faithfulness to last longer than just a "morning dew" (See vss. 4-6). The relationship between God and His wife was not easy! It was very one-sided in that the wife (Israel) was very unpredictable while God remained the same.

God's trait of faithfulness is very important for you in your new world. You must persistently be proactive in taking your place in your *new* world. You must continue, and act faithfully. Continue doing the right thing regardless of how others may act! That's the character of God that you need to mirror!

The story of Hosea and Gomer is actually more about the merciful loving character of God and his sterling character of persistent faithfulness than about marriage and divorce. God would not give up because He loved his people! This is a story about God's steadfast love, his continued perseverance, His persistent faithfulness even in the face of unfaithfulness and failure. In this story we are reminded of one of the basic tenets of our faith: *Our God is a loving, forgiving God who believes in us even if we continually fail Him!*

This often-conflicted relationship of Hosea and Gomer teaches us many things about faithfulness. Divine faith functions through such traits as mercy, concern, patience and forgiveness. Nowhere are these traits more essential than for those seeking the restoration of their faith when they are single, *again*! Successful restoration of faith and faithfulness must be patterned after the faithfulness of God.

Biblical marriage, as you will remember, is a platform where the spiritual discipline of perseverance is best developed. It is, in fact, the linchpin-relationship that holds our society together. Thus, the dissolution of your marriage probably challenged your faith in everything! You begin to question other things you thought were true. You probably feel overwhelmed by your *questions* pertaining to what is right and wrong!

Your other covenant fellow-travelers feel the same way! Now is a time to faithfully stand your ground on your core beliefs. Now is a time to gain stability, not chaos. Rather than questioning what you think you *do not* believe, focus on the things *you do* believe.

Read 1 Timothy 4:1-16

In this passage God warns us to watch out for those who will deceive us with hypocrisy. Don't listen to them. It is much easier to inject doubt as an agnostic than it is to pursue truth and become a believer. Many people will tell you what *you should or should not* do. Some will even try to speak *for God*! Just be sure it is God speaking and not some man's opinion or supposed logic. Trust in the living God (vs. 10).

This passage encourages us to "exercise to godliness" (vss. 7-8). You will only save yourself by *"taking heed to yourself and your teaching...continue in them"* (vs. 16). Take some time for self-examination and to accumulate additional information, then race toward your *new normal!* Yes, there is a race to be won, ---and you are still in it!

FAITH AND THE NEW NORMAL

Marriages are supposed to last a long time...a *lifetime!* Being single, *again* or remarried your life has been turned upside down! God's structure for biblical marriage with dependent and independent roles provides our desired stability. Usually the longer a marriage lasts, the more stable it becomes. If that marriage ends, our desire then is to re-stabilize our lives.

READ Hebrews 12:1-3

Yes, you must be tired of running! Following the ordeal you have gone through you are tempted to just find a place and hide! Perseverance, *patient endurance, ---faithfulness!* ...will give you the ability to finish your race! It is hard. It is a challenge to face all the others that are in your race. Courage is what you need. Look to Jesus who, according to this passage is the *"author and finisher"* of your race!

In addition, this entire chapter (Hebrews 12) outlines the process of restoring and rebuilding your faith and faithfulness. Here is an exercise in spiritual discipline, patient endurance...faithfulness! Note these points from the text:

- *Look around for people who will "en-courage" you.* A loving family and true friends form the social network you need. Now is *not* the time to be alienated from those who love you.

- *Lay aside things that burden (worry) you.* Do what you can to make it right, but don't be anxious over the things beyond your control.
- *Look to Jesus to coach you...and listen to Him!* God speaks to us through his written word. Go to the Bible for your answers, don't accept conventional wisdom! Trust your ability to understand God's will for yourself. I repeat: "BE YOUR OWN PRIEST."
- *Don't let your troubles (disciplining from the Lord) discourage you.* Life is a series of choices. You have made some wrong choices. Chastening consequences resulted from those choices. Discipline is not joyous, but in the end it is helpful.
- *Live your life for the peaceful fruit of righteousness and godliness* (vs.11). The rest of your life is no less a matter of choices than what's gone before. Choose carefully the things and the people that will produce peace and godliness.
- *Make peace with all men to avoid bitterness.* You *can not* dwell on old wrongs. When you are the victim of vicious sins, forgiveness is the only choice you have to ward off bitterness and hate. You must "*seek peace and pursue it*" with all men (1 Peter 3:11)

Ideal marriages are based on the model of God's faithfulness. During times of crisis an enduring *persistent love* similar to God's love is needed. Such persistence serves to stabilize us. Biblical marriage tends to put things in place. Solid marriages make life orderly and predictable! In some ways when you became single, *again* you lost that stability of life. Your current instability (married, then single, *again* or possibly remarried!) is both a time of danger and opportunity. Many bad things can happen if you blindly try to steady the boat by jumping into another marriage! On the other hand, this is an ideal time for you to actually start your life over! Today truly is "the first day of the rest of your life"!

The Apostle Paul focuses the goal you must have during these turbulent times with these words (God gives) *"eternal life to those who by patient continuance in doing good seek for glory, honor, and immortality* "(Romans 2:6-7).

This goal of patient continuance, the spiritual discipline of faithfulness, has meaning only for those who have developed a clear sense of eternity. Seeing *eternity* in time is the focus of faith in the future. In fact, your interest in biblical marriage is important only because you believe in *life* beyond this life. Your faith provides the ability for you to see the future. But, you *must* have faith! For *without faith it is impossible to please Him, for he who comes to God must believe that He is, and that He is a rewarder of those who diligently seek Him."* (Hebrews 11:6)

PRACTICING TO PREDICT THE FUTURE

Your *faith* provides you with a telescope to look into the future, but it is based on your knowledge of the Word of God and your experiences of faith from the past! The beauty of this is that you can actually practice your faith to predict your future, by practicing your past *faith*! In other words, get busy doing the things of faith that you know and love from your past life…like praying, reading the scriptures, talking about what you believe, and engaging in worship to God!

READ **Hebrews 11:1-2**

When you became single, *again* many things changed in your life. Things like where you live, how you see life, and even the people with whom you associate, including your friends! Your economic lifestyle probably changed as well, usually for the worse rather than the better! Perhaps you had to take on a new job just to make the ends meet. Some of the more frivolous changes might include that new tattoo, or the motorcycle out in the garage! Things are different, and your life *has* changed!

Although many things have changed, some things have *not* changed. You can depend on God's love and faithfulness just like before. Nothing can separate you from the love of God (Romans 8:8-9). God loved you even while you were not faithful to Him (Romans 5:8). Why would you expect anything less now? The steadfast love of the Lord *never* ceases! That you can depend on!

In addition, the people in your faith-fellowship have not changed. The restoration of *your faith* in God could be implemented through His people! Yes, God's people have often had detractors, even betrayers (Matthew 26:14-15 Judas Iscariot!) among them. In fact, 'men of the cloth" (Matthew 27:1-2 – religious leaders!) may stand out as enemies of what is right and good. However, multitudes of good people of faith as loving souls are compassionate toward those who are broken (See Philippians1; I Corinthians 5; 2 Corinthians 2:5-11). This also you can depend upon!

Faith in Yourself

You are probably questioning other things as well. You may feel more vulnerable to making mistakes now than before. After our son's painful divorce I was helping him move his few belongings in a rental truck through the rush hour traffic of Atlanta. As fathers are prone to do, I was telling him how to drive when he blurted out: "Dad, at least I still know how to drive a truck!" My offer to give driving advice actually made him even more aware of his shattered confidence and self-worth. I did not help him by challenging his confidence in himself.

READ 2 Timothy 1:12-13

Your personal confidence and faith must be restored. You need the confidence of the Apostle Paul: *"for I know whom I   have believed , and am persuaded that he is able to keep that which I have committed unto him against that day "*.

This is a good time to take a *correct* inventory of your knowledge and abilities. Look to your past faith experiences with God. This could include such things as going to worship, helping the needy, or visiting the sick and elderly. Your faith in yourself springs from an honest informed heart. The decisions you are called upon to make now must be based on facts, *not* wishful thinking! Now is when you need to be able to say *"I know whom I have believed....!"* Trust God, *and* believe in yourself.

Faith in Others

Rejection means: "a refusal to accept, approve; a refusal to show someone the love or kindness that they need or expect; the feeling that someone does not love or want you" (Macmillian Dictionary). Rejection is hard for a young child being bullied on the playground by another 12-year old, but it can be emotionally crippling for those single, *again*! You might have felt completely worthless and incompetent due to rejection you have felt, even from close friends and relatives. The wise words of Solomon ring true: *"Death and life is in the power of the tongue, and they that love it will eat its fruit"* (Proverbs 18:21).

Faith in "the Faith"

The fact that you have read this far in this book indicates that your Christian faith (corporate or personal) is very important to you. You are interested in biblical marriage. We have tried to emphasize that above all else, you must believe and do what will be pleasing to God. The Bible says this about "the faith":

> *Mercy, peace, and love be multiplied to you. Beloved, while I was very diligent to write to you concerning our common salvation, I found it necessary to write to you exhorting you to contend earnestly for the faith which was once for all delivered to the saints* (Jude 2-3).

You could use this passage as an outline for restoring your faith in "the faith". First, you will need to show *mercy*, practice *peace* and demonstrate *love* for your brothers and sisters of faith. In the process of a divorce, mistakes are made by many individuals. Harsh words were spoken. Rejection was certainly felt! Mercy, peace and love are essential to your recovery.

Second, you must realize that it *is* a matter of *salvation*. Many single, *again* saints reject their faith. They might have dropped out because of the bad memories, or even because of the good ones that remind them of their past. My wife's brother dropped out of his local church for a short time following the death of his beloved wife because it brought back so many memories. Others might leave the church because of the shame and guilt they feel. Shame and guilt may serve to call us to repentance and forgiveness. Others leave because they just do not feel welcome in the place (church) where their faith was practiced. Perhaps the occasions of worship became the battleground for their divorce issues. Nonetheless, how you recover or maintain your faith is a matter of the salvation of your soul.

Third, Jude says our *faith* is worth the time and effort required to "*contend earnestly*" for it! Keep one thing in mind: our God is a loving God who desires that we should be saved rather than be lost. That salvation is housed in "*the faith*" we practice. Never let anyone or anything separate you from your faith! What you believe and how you practice it is the most important part of your spiritual recovery following the loss of your mate.

PRACTICE FOR THE FUTURE

Daddy was in his late 80's when mother died and their marriage of more than six decades ended...or, at least ended on earth. Moments after mother passed, Daddy leaned over her bed, gently kissed her and said, *"I'll be along soon!"* He could not imagine a future in this life without his soul-mate of 60-plus years! But, then again he did not expect to have six more years on earth without her!

The future seems like a very lonely place for those who are single, *again*. God's design for marriage from the beginning was to dispel loneliness. In marriage two people share the most intimate experiences. Christians particularly see their relationship to each other as a tandem-team designed to do the work of God on earth! The loneliness is deadening to the point that when asked about "the future", you might respond: "What future!"

What *should you be doing* to prepare for living in your new world of being single, *again*? The Bible does not give definitive step-by-step instructions, but it does provide a good process to practice in Hebrews 12:12-16

> *Therefore, <u>strengthen</u> your tired arms and your weak knees, and make <u>straight paths</u> for your feet, so that what is lame may not become worse but rather be healed. <u>Pursue peace</u> with everyone, as well as <u>holiness</u>, without which no one will see the Lord. See to it that no one fails to obtain the grace of God and that <u>no bitter</u> root grows up and causes you trouble, or many of you will become defiled. No one should be <u>immoral or godless.</u>*

How do you *practice* for the future? The key principles are outlined in this Scripture:

1) *Be strong* (Build yourself up with spiritual exercise.)
2) *Make a plan* (Make spiritual decisions about your future.)
3) *Pursue peace* (Fix what can be fixed; forgive, start over.)
4) *Be holy* (Be *right* with God)
5) *Avoid bitterness* (Forgiveness is the only way this is possible!)
6) *Avoid immorality and godlessness* (Maintain a life of purity.)

Yes, you do have a future! It must be lived in a world quite different from the past, but your future *does not* have to depend on your past. It is a *brave* new world that will call for courage, confidence and a strong faith.   God forgives, but it is up to you to turn from what's wrong, accept his forgiveness and move on. No one else can do it for you.

The final chapter focuses on the question you will probably ask either now or later: *"Should I marry again?"* Your answer to this question will depend on your search for the truth and on the conclusions you have drawn from your personal situation. The statistical fact is, you *will* more than likely want to marry again.

Chapter 10

REMARRIAGE:

SHOULD I MARRY AGAIN!?

Seeker's Task #10: Continue to be "God's Image" for His world!

> *You have now come full circle! Your first "Seeker's task" was to* <u>*become*</u> *a super-saint. This is another way of saying, "Be as good a Christian as you can be!" Your final task for the rest of your life is your commitment to* <u>*be*</u> *such a super-saint!*

Tom and Patsy were childhood sweethearts who had been married for more than twenty-five years. Their marriage was stormy from the very beginning, but as Christians they did not believe in divorce! Together they had endured nearly three decades of marital discord rather than marital bliss while producing three beautiful children. Economically, they had become financially successful, but that did not translate into marital success. Both Tom and Patsy accused each other of having violated their vows. Though she admitted to not being the best wife, Patsy had stayed with Tom through several affairs and had extended forgiveness multiple times. However, over time the trust of the marriage eroded. They divorced. Some years later, this dear friend wrote the following letter. This is not an exact quote of the actual letter[62], but the gist of it said:

Dear G. R.:

As you know, I tried to make my marriage work, but Tom made that impossible. I stayed with him for many years because of the children. Truthfully, I loved him in spite of himself. And, I believed our marriage was supposed to be for life! But, I finally had to call it quits, and leave him. It was the hardest thing I have ever done.

Now I am forced to move on. I have met someone who genuinely cares for me. He is a good person and has asked me to marry him. Do you think I should accept his offer and marry again?

Love, Patsy

This letter epitomizes the intent of this book. Our desire is to help good people (…especially those who are divorced and single, *again!*) seek out the <u>*right*</u> (biblical) definition of "marriage" for them. The "Tom and Patsy marriage/ divorce/remarriage" dilemma in general and Patsy's letter in particular encapsulates many of the issues single, *again* Christians' must face.

1) *Patsy sincerely wanted to do it right regarding remarriage after a divorce!*

It would be a mistake to judge her decisions and actions

by impugning her motives. Individuals who find themselves single-*again* following the security they knew in a previous marriage are often in a double-bind! They *do* want to be *married but* they *don't* want to be … MARRIED! The question *"Should I remarry?"* is an honest inquiry from a genuinely sincere heart. Patsy did not want a repeat performance like her previous marriage, but she also was frightened at the thought of living single. Biblical marriage after divorce was an important topic for her. She honestly wanted to do the right thing!

2) *When Patsy contemplated remarriage she understood that marriage/divorce issues are not simple, but very complex!*

Yet, she probably thought that her story was unique…one of a kind! According to traditional wisdom, she appeared to have *scriptural cause* for divorce: *sexual immorality*. Tom had had many affairs! He admitted it. But, on the other hand, she had granted forgiveness to Tom for his sexual unfaithfulness…*more than once!* In fact, the actual divorce did not result from the sin of sexual immorality, but from the overall long-time situation of the marriage! Patsy was just tired and now that the children were grown, the decision to divorce was easier. The complexity of the answers that came from her friends and also from religious experts only compounded her dilemma. Nothing about it was simple for her. Truthfully, Patsy wanted somebody else to make her decisions for her.

3) *Patsy knew that her marriage did not breakdown overnight by a sudden single cause even though she was urged to identify one!*

In fact, she would probably have had trouble pointing to a single event or time to date the marriage failure. She *could* inventory many of her grievances that contributed to the divorce! In fact, those painful memories (…and even the good memories!) may answer the question for her about whether or not she should marry again.

4) *Patsy reached out for help from others.*

The one thing she knew *for sure* was that she did not know *anything* "for sure"!   The turbulence in the wake of a divorce often drowns the survivors in negative emotions of anger, guilt, and un-forgiveness. The usual tendency is to reach out to others, grabbing whatever seems stable and solid. Most of us believe we know some things as a matter of fact, and are more than willing to express our confidence to those who ask. However, asking someone else to make the decision for you about whether or not you should remarry is understandable, but futile!

Since everyone in your circle has a vested interest in how you answer that question, you will get numerous answers. There is no shortage of experts trying to either tell you or to coerce you to do what they think is the right thing. It is natural for us to turn to friends, family, and faith-leaders when we are making difficult decisions. However, just remember: It is *your* decision!

5) *Patsy's desire to do it right prompted her to solicit a religious answer from a trusted minister-friend.*

Patsy's faith and her religious beliefs were always very important for her. Undoubtedly, a major piece of her decision would be based on "the faith" she contended for, and on the people who represented it. But, the answers she might get could force her to choose between her faith and her new love.

It *is useful* to examine *all* information and directions that will help you decide, including conventional wisdom advice, professional counseling, and guidance from those of your religious faith!   As we have noted, however, let God speak to you through a thorough study of the scriptures. Do not walk away from your *faith*, or the God of your Faith!

LIVING SINGLE, *AGAIN*

Having said that, there are some predictable problems you may face while living single, not the least of which is the threat of sexual immorality! Sexual relations are critically important as a function of our divine creation. However, acceptable sexual relations before God are *restricted* to those between the two partners in a biblical marriage. Paul, the apostle of Christ, urged Christians to respect the sexual rights of their marital partners (I Corinthians 7:4-5) by *"not defrauding"* (rejecting) such activities. The *"marriage bed is undefiled"* (Hebrews 13:4). It is right, acceptable before God, for a husband and wife to engage in sexual activities with each other.

The greatest threat is engaging in sex which is sinful while living single. Human beings are divinely created with the innate need for sexual satisfaction. Two guards against this threat are: a strong spiritual commitment to celibacy and natural aging. Sexual immorality may not be as threatening for an older person who chooses to live single as it would be for a younger person. This need does tend to decline as a person grows older. Paul's admonition to Timothy (1 Timothy 5:3-14) about widows indicates this difference. Older widows were to be supported while younger widows were commanded *to marry*. The reason stated was that the younger widows would become *"wanton"* (KJV). The New International Version translates this phrase: *"when their sensual desires overcome their dedication to Christ, they want to marry"*.

Re-READ I Corinthians 7:1-40

This is a very important passage for those divorced or

remarried. In this passage five relatively common situations are defined regarding biblical marriage and sexual relations:

1) *Celibate single: deciding not to marry with the power to control sexual desires:*

These were religious celibates who had taken the vow of purity. Paul placed himself in this category stating that he wished everyone could control their sexual urges as dedicated celibates (vss. 1, 9-10)

2) *A typical marriage of a man (husband) and a woman (wife):*

The prevailing command is that they owe it to each other to provide sexual satisfaction within the marriage. (vss. 2-6).

3) *The previously married, un-married (divorcees and widows):*

Paul indicated that it would be better not to (*re*)-marry until reconciliation was impossible, particularly during the "*present distress*". Certain types of difficult times are *more* difficult on married Christians than on those who are single.

4) *A mixed marriage of a believer and a un-believer.*

The (Christian) believer's goal should be to perform the duties of marriage; however, if the unbeliever "departs", (divorces, abandons, separates from) the believer, then he/she is not "bound" any longer. (Vss. 12-17).

5) *Virgins and widows, singles who are not religious celibates,:*

Stay single if you can control your sexual desires, but otherwise you are free to marry "in the Lord". (vss. 25-40)

The basic instruction is clear: Biblical marriage is the

only proper state for those who desire to be sexually active. This instruction pertains to the first marriage or to any subsequent *re*-marriage following divorce or death. If you choose to remain single, a key element pertaining to your spiritual relationship with God is whether or not you can control your sexual impulses to remain sexually pure. Remarriage may be your most appropriate option.

SEEK *FIRST* THE KINGDOM OF GOD

"Seek first the Kingdom of God and His righteousness" (Matthew 6:33) remains the guiding principle in any biblical marriage. Sincere seekers after the truth will want God's approval, particularly regarding a *re*-marriage. Thus, the only course of action open to the Christian is to humbly submit to the will of God. This is a daunting task for anyone, but especially when you are considering remarriage following a divorce. However, the promise of God is clear:

> *"Ask, and it will be given to you; seek, and you will find; knock, and it will be opened to you.* (Matthew 7:7). Jesus said it best: *Come to Me, all you who labor and are heavy laden, and I will give you rest.* (Matthew 11:28).

The question of a biblical remarriage for any Christian is critically argued by the scholars and passionately defended with both negative and positive results. There are those who would say *no one* for *any reason* may *remarry* following a divorce.[63] Others would argue that remarriage is both implied and possible for anyone following a divorce if repentance and forgiveness are evident.[64] The traditional view is that remarriage is acceptable for the innocent party in cases of sexual immorality, but not the "guilty" party.[65] Still other scholars would allow a person to remarry if the divorce was for other reasons in addition to sexual immorality[66]. There is certainly a "multitude of counselors" on this topic!

Several resources are provided in the back of this book for your further study. As a sincere seeker you will want to examine the various scholarly commentators and their conclusions; however, your final faith-action must come from your personal study of God's Word. God will bless your sincere efforts, and you will be able to make a righteous decision.

However, there are some questions that might help guide your decision about whether or not another marriage is right for you. Here is a limited list of vital questions you might consider:

1) What did I contribute to the divorce?
2) What did I learn about myself from it?
3) Have I confessed my wrongdoing to God and others?
4) What am I doing to keep from letting whatever hurtful attitudes, habits, actions creep into my current relationships of all kinds *and* to become more Christ-like?
5) Can I be satisfied with friends, family, children and other non-sexual relationships as I remain single?
6) Why do I want to remarry--what are my motives?
7) What do I hope to get from this marriage?
8) What am I willing to give to this marriage?
9) What do I most fear when I think about remarriage?
10) What impediments will I face if I remarry and what will I need to do to overcome them if I do remarry?
11) How will this remarriage affect my other fellow-travelers such as my children, my parents, church friends, etc.?
12) What changes will a remarriage make in my life? ...my religious faith!

My answer to Patsy was probably not what she wanted to hear, it may even sound cold and uncaring, but in all good conscience it was the *only answer* I could give: *"Patsy, with God's help you must decide for yourself!"* In the end, like Patsy you are the only one who can answer the question "Should I marry again?"

The information in this book is most applicable to those of you who are single, *again* because of divorce. Since the theme is biblical marriage, a remarried person must also decide whether or not his/her remarriage is in fact a *biblical marriage.* But, before you break up another marriage by divorce be very sure it is what God wants you to do. How you live now as a Christian is critical. Truthfully, you cannot be a super saint! We know that, but you must set your goal to be as good a disciple as possible.

The Bible does give a definite goal for you to pursue. You should be the best example of a Christian possible! What you are seeking for a way to live is outlined in the following verses.

Re-READ Colossians 3:5-15

Put to death, therefore, whatever belongs to your earthly nature: sexual immorality, impurity, lust, evil desires and greed, which is idolatry. 6 Because of these, the wrath of God is coming. 7 You used to walk in these ways, in the life you once lived. 8 But now you must rid yourselves of all such things as these: anger, rage, malice, slander, and filthy language from your lips. 9 Do not lie to each other, since you have taken off your old self with its practices 10 and have put on the new self, which is being renewed in knowledge in the image of its Creator. 11 Here there is no Greek or Jew, circumcised or uncircumcised, barbarian, Scythian, slave or free, but Christ is all, and is in all. 12 Therefore, as God's chosen people, holy and dearly loved, clothe yourselves with compassion, kindness, humility, gentleness and patience. 13 Bear with each other and forgive whatever grievances you may have against one another. Forgive as the Lord forgave you. 14 And over all these virtues put on love, which binds them all together in perfect unity. 15 Let the peace of Christ rule in your hearts, since as members of one body you were called to peace. And be thankful. (New International Version NIV)

Trust in the love and forgiveness of God. Remember, you and you alone must answer to Him! Then, trust in yourself and your ability to study God's Word and to obey it to the best of your ability. .

EPILOGUE

In the early 1970's Dr. James O. Baird approached this author about speaking on the topic *"How Should the Church Address the Problem of Marriage, Divorce and Remarriage?"* at the Oklahoma Christian College annual lectureship. He said he wanted a "fresh mind", a person who had not published or was not well-known on the topic. As the young preacher for a strong church in Eastern Oklahoma where the issues were recently addressed, he believed I could do it. There was just one major problem! I knew I had very limited knowledge of the topic even though for more than a decade I had had to deal with it in my ministry. But, I was "fresh" and I had a year to prepare! Little did I know that the topic would become such a major part of my ministry over the ensuing years?

Back then the ministers of the area came together on Tuesdays to fellowship and discuss mutual ministerial problems. I thought, what better place to study "How the church addresses the problem of marriage, divorce and remarriage" than in these ministers' meetings. They agreed to allow some of those Tuesdays for discussion and research on what they called "my topic" (with a sinister laugh!). I knew this was a controversial topic, but I had no idea it was as *p-a-s-s-i-o-n-a-t-l-y* contradictory as it was among these ministers!

Each of the ministers, from the seasoned warriors of the Cross to the red-cheeked novices defended his position with fervor. The information I gleaned from the "Tuesday meetings" and from my broader in-depth study was presented at OC the following year.

Why am I telling you this? First, to let you know that you are not alone if you are confused about what you should or should not do regarding marriage issues? Just a cursory review of the "Resources for Further Study" will show that the best minds among us differ on various parts of this topic. It has been more than four decades since I prepared to speak at OC. There has been little progress made during that time in reducing the number of marriages that fail. Sincere ministers are still asking "How should the church address the problem of marriage, divorce and remarriage?" Each is honestly seeking an answer to this troubling issue.

Second, I want to reinforce what this book is all about: *You have to decide for yourself!* That is why I have given numerous Scriptures for you to read for yourself. Salvation and being "Okay with God" is a very personal matter! It is okay to seek-out commentaries, recommendations, and other information you need; but, ultimately it is your life, your soul, and your salvation! Leaning on a multitude of counselors may not only be confusing, but may also be very dangerous.

Third, only God knows everything about you, your mate, your marriage and your divorce. A man's acceptance or rejection of you or your marriage does not make it right or wrong. Only God knows the truth about your marriage. Only God can look into your heart and discern your "intents" and your motivations. God's acceptance is the only acceptance that is truly important for you. Seek God's Will, and by faith obey it! Remember, God is a forgiving God.

As I stated in the *Introduction* this book is not intended to defend any position on any part of the controversies over biblical marriage. In fact, my attempt to capsulize various positions in short sentences is very inadequate and may even leave an incorrect conclusion. Even though I have tried to be fair and accurate, you are encouraged to study the questions that pertain to your situation in the original works in the "Resources for Further Study" section of this book.

My purpose has been to offer encouragement to those of you who are single, *again*. You should not be made to feel like you are a second-class citizen in the Kingdom of God. Those of us in positions of religious leadership should be the first to welcome you as a sincere seeker after truth. We all must act with the compassion and accept the forgiveness of our Lord. None of us has the right or obligation *on our own* to speak or act for God. All of us must be conscientiously bound by the written word of God, and be subject to His divine justice, mercy, and forgiveness.

Nonetheless, there are a few principles about biblical marriage that I am compelled by my own convictions to present to you for your consideration.

- *Biblical marriage is God's plan for intimate relationship between a committed man and a committed woman that is protected by vows of faithfulness.*

- *Biblical marriage should be entered into by a man and a woman for life.*

- *Biblical marriage forms the core of the Christian family where children can be most adequately reared and trained for service to God.*

- *Divorce is really bad and should always be the very last option any couple uses to solve the problems of sin in a bad marriage.*

- *All biblical marriages are truly "made in heaven" in terms of definition, duration, and termination. As a just and loving God, He alone will judge the validity of any marriage.*

These are very general statements about my faith. They do not detail some of the things I conclude as matters of opinion. These general statements of belief are offered in the hope of giving you a workable framework to investigate many of the more complex issues you face. May God bless you in your search for the truth on biblical marriage. (GRH)

ENDNOTES

Chapter 1 - Where Do I go from Here?

[1] This is not to disparage language analyses of the original texts. Any student of the Bible knows that something can be lost in translation. You are encouraged to study the theological references as well as the therapeutic references.

[2] For example, note the reference edited by H. Wayne House, *Divorce and Remarriage: Four Christian Views,* or, the *Divorce Debate* between Hicks and Waldron.

[3] The Old Testament practice of celibacy was usually due to "a divine gift" of "undivided devotion to the Lord" as described by Kostenberger in *God, Marriage and the Family,* pp.173-182.

Chapter 2 - Seeking the Ideal Biblical Marrige

[4] Smoke, Jim (1995). *Growing Through Divorce,* Harvest House Publishers, Eugene, OR., p.9

[5] From Website, "Losing a mate: Life after death of a spouse"

[6] Thomas, J. D. (1977). Divorce and Remarriage, Biblical

Research Press, 774 East North 15th St, Abilene, TX 79601, p.4

[7] Showers, Renald E., (1983) *Lawfully wedded: What constitutes marriage in the sight of God?* Philadelphia College of the Bible, p.36

[8] Kostenberger, Andreas J. (2004).*God, Marriage and the Family: Rebuilding Biblical Foundations*, Crossway Books, Wheaton, IL. Pp.42-49

[9] Thomas, Gary, (2000) *Sacred Marriage.* Zondervan, Grand Rapids, MI. p.265

[10] Atkinson, David, (1981). *To Have and to Hold*, Eerdman Press, New York, NY. P.75

[11] Thomas, Gary, (2000) *Sacred Marriage.* Zondervan, Grand Rapids, MI. P.33

Chapter 3 - God Knew He Needed her

[12] Lowery, Fred, (2002) *Covenant Marriage: Staying Together for Life*, Howard Books, 1230 Avenue of the Americas, New York, NY 10020. P. 143

[13] Ibid. Lowery, p. 145

[14] Gottman, John, (1994) Why Marriages Suceeed or Fail. Simon and Schuester, New York, New York, p. 13.

[15]Instone-Brewer, David (2002). Divorce and Remarriage in the Bible, The Social and Literary Context, William B. Eerdmans Publishing Company, Grand Rapids, MI. Pp.213-237.

[16] Ibid., Instone-Brewer, p.222

[17] Ibid., Instone-Brewer, p. 254

[18] Thomas, Gary, (2000) Sacred Marriage. Zondervan, Grand Rapids, MI., p.201

Chapter 4 - Biblical Marriage: Created in the Image of God

[19] Selected from song, "Father's World" by Maltbie Babcock, *Praise the Lord Hymnal,* Praise Press, Nashville, TN. 37204, John P. Wiegard., Ed.

[20] Kostenberger, Andreas J. (2004).*God, Marriage and the Family: Rebuilding Biblical Foundations,* Crossway Books, Wheaton, IL. P. 93

[21] Thomas, Gary, (2000) *Sacred Marriage.* Zondervan, Grand Rapids, MI.p. 13

[22] Ibid., Thomas, Gary as quoted from Mary Ann McPherson Oliver, *Conjugal Spirituality: The Primacy of Mutual Love in Christian Tradition,* P. 33

[23] Ibid., Thomas, Gary, Index

[24] Ibid., Thomas, Gary, p. 265

[25] Lowery, Fred, (2002) Covenant Marriage: Staying Together for Life, Howard Books, 1230 Avenue of the Americas, New York, NY 10020. P. 225-226.

Chapter 5 - Divorce: Worse than Death?

[26] Frisbie, David and Lisa (2006). *Moving Forward After Divorce,*

Harvest House Publishers, Eugene, OR. P. 204

[27]From www.divorcerarte.org website

[28]From www.pewsocialtrends.org. website

[29]Instone-Brewer, David (2002). *Divorce and Remarriage in the Bible, The Social and Literary Context*, William B. Eerdmans Publishing Company, Grand Rapids, MI. Pp.241-258

[30]House, H. Wayne Ed, (1990). *Divorce and Remarriage: Four Christian Views,* Inter-Varsity Press, Downers Grove, IL. P. 48

Chapter 6 Divorce: Biblical Grounds

[31]Instone-Brewer, David (2003). *Divorce and Remarriage in the Church, Biblical Solutions for Pastoral Realities.* Intervarsity Press, Downers Grove, Illinois 60515-1426m p. 54.

[32]Layfield, Lavelle, (2003) *When Marriages Bomb there is a Balm in Jesus Christ*, LayMar Publishers, 111 Penny Lane, Athens, TX 75751-3247.p. 38

[33]Instone-Brewer, David (2002). *Divorce and Remarriage in the Bible, The Social and Literary Context*, William B. Eerdmans Publishing Company, Grand Rapids, MI. Pp.133-167.

[34]House, H. Wayne Ed, (1990). *Divorce and Remarriage: Four Christian Views,* Inter-Varsity Press, Downers Grove, IL. P. 151

[35]Thomas, J. D. (1977). *Divorce and Remarriage,* Biblical Research Press, 774 East North 15th St, Abilene, TX 79601. P. 7

[36]Schubert, Joe D. (1966). *Marriage, Divorce and Purity.* Biblical

Research Press, 774 East North 15th Street, Abilene, Texas 79601. P. 55

[37]Keener, S., (2007) ...*and Marries Another: Divorce and Remarriage in the Teachings of the New Testament,* Hendrickson Publishers, Inc. P. O. Box 3473, Peabody, MA 01961-3473. P.56

[38]Shelly, Rubel, (2007). *Divorce and Remarriage: A Redemptive Theology.* Leafwood Publishers, Abilene, TX. P. 126

[39]Instone-Brewer, David (2002). *Divorce and Remarriage in the Bible, The Social and Literary Context,* William B. Eerdmans Publishing Company, Grand Rapids, MI.Pp.128-9

[40]Ibid., p.100

[41]Instone-Brewer, David (2003). *Divorce and Remarriage in the Church, Biblical Solutions for Pastoral Realities.* Intervarsity Press, Downers Grove, Illinois 60515-1426 Pp. 35-39

[42]Shelly, Rubel, (2007). *Divorce and Remarriage: A Redemptive Theology.* Leafwood Publishers, Abilene, TX. P. 54

[43]Kostenberger, Andreas J. (2004).*God, Marriage and the Family: Rebuilding Biblical Foundations,* Crossway Books, Wheaton, IL.

[44]Shelly, Rubel, (2007). *Divorce and Remarriage: A Redemptive Theology.* Leafwood Publishers, Abilene, TX. P. 138

[45]Layfield, Lavelle, (2003) *When Marriages Bomb there is a Balm in Jesus Christg,* LayMar Publishers, 111 Penny Lane, Athens, TX 75751-3247. P.39

[46]Keener, S., (2007) ...*and Marries Another: Divorce and Remarriage in the Teachings of the New Testament,* Hendrickson

Publishers, Inc. P. O. Box 3473, Peabody, MA 01961-3473. P. 105

[47]Instone-Brewer, David (2002). *Divorce and Remarriage in the Bible, The Social and Literary Context,* William B. Eerdmans Publishing Company, Grand Rapids, MI. P. 85

[48]Shelly, Rubel, (2007). *Divorce and Remarriage: A Redemptive Theology.* Leafwood Publishers, Abilene, TX. P. 115

Chapter 7 - Forgiveness

[49] Smoke, Jim (1995). *Growing Through Divorce,* Harvest House Publishers, Eugene, OR.Pp. 90-93.

[50] Shelly, Rubel, (2007). *Divorce and Remarriage: A Redemptive Theology.* Leafwood Publishers, Abilene, TX. P.150.

[51] Instone-Brewer, David (2003). *Divorce and Remarriage in the Church, Biblical Solutions for Pastoral Realities.* Intervarsity Press, Downers Grove, Illinois 60515-1426. P. 191.

Chapter 8 - Spiritual Recovery: The Next Right Turn

[52] Our grandson, Matt, found himself in a troubled marriage where doubt, abuse, and unfaithfulness were too common. He loved his children and tried to make it work. There were other options that could have solved his problems, including divorce as a last resort; but for reasons unknown to all of us, he ended it by taking his own life.

[53] Thomas, J. D. (1977). *Divorce and Remarriage,* Biblical Research Press, 774 East North 15th St, Abilene, TX 79601. P. 57.

[54] J. Carl Laney in House, H. Wayne Ed, (1990). *Divorce and*

Remarriage: Four Christian Views, Inter-Varsity Press, Downers Grove, IL., p. 48.

[55]Larry Richards in House, H. Wayne Ed, (1990). *Divorce and Remarriage: Four Christian Views,* Inter-Varsity Press, Downers Grove, IL. pp. 241-5

[56] Keener, S., (2007) *...and Marries Another: Divorce and Remarriage in the Teachings of the New Testament,* Hendrickson Publishers, Inc. P. O. Box 3473, Peabody, MA 01961-3473. P. 106.

[57] Shelly, Rubel, (2007). *Divorce and Remarriage: A Redemptive Theology.* Leafwood Publishers, Abilene, TX.

[58] Smoke, Jim (1995). *Growing Through Divorce,* Harvest House Publishers, Eugene, OR.

[59]Byron Brown is a respected English professor, my fellow-church leader, and a good friend. He has an acute ability to place things in their proper places. Sometimes what may seem to be the safest place (a foxhole) may in fact become a grave. His illustration vividly shows why you need to move on!

Chapter 9 - Restoring Faith and Faithfulness

[60] Frisbie, David and Lisa (2006). *Moving Forward After Divorce,* Harvest House Publishers, Eugene, OR. P. 9.

[61] Thomas, Gary, (2000) *Sacred Marriage.* Zondervan, Grand Rapids, MI. P. 104

Chapter 10 - Remarriage…Should I marry again?

[62] Tom and Patsy were two of our dearest friends. Their

children were good friends with our children. Our families were very close. That's made it difficult to advise Patsy on what to do?

[63] Strauss, Mark L., Gordon J. Wenham, William A. Heth, and Craig S. Keener (2006). *Remarriage After Divorce in Today's Church: Three Views,* Zondervan, Grand Rapids, MI. Pp. 19-49.

[64] Ibid., p. 111.

[65] Thomas, J. D. (1977). *Divorce and Remarriage,* Biblical Research Press, 774 East North 15th St, Abilene, TX 79601. Pp. 53-58

[66] House, H. Wayne Ed, (1990). *Divorce and Remarriage: Four Christian Views,* Inter-Varsity Press, Downers Grove, IL. Pp.215-249

RESOURCES FOR FURTHER STUDY

Adams, Jay E. (1980). *Marriage Divorce and Remarriage*, Zondervan, Grand Rapids, Michigan, 49530.

Adams, Jay E. (1983). *Solving Marriage Problems, Biblical Solutions for Christian Counselors,* Zondervan, Grand Rapids, MI 49530.

Adams, Jay E., (1986).*How to Help People Change: The Four-Step Process,* Zondervan, Grand Rapids, Michigan, 49530

Atkinson, David, (1981). *To Have and to Hold,* Eerdman Press, New York, NY

Batchelor, Doug (2011). *The Bible on Marriage, Divorce and Remarriage*, Amazing Facts, P. O. Box 1058, Roseville, CA.

Deasley, Alex R. G. (2000). *Marriage and Divorce in the Bible and the Church.* Beacon Hill Press, Kansas City, KS.

Eldredge, Robert Sr. (2002). *Can Divorced Christians Marry?* Choice Publications, P. O. Box 132, Camarillo, CA

Frisbie, David and Lisa (2006). *Moving Forward After Divorce,* Harvest House Publishers, Eugene, OR.

Gola, Stephen, (2005). *Divorce: God's Will*, Holy Fire Publishing, 531 Constitution Blvd, Martinsburg, WV 25401.

Gottman, John, (1994) *Why Marriages Suceeed or Fail.* Simon and Schuester, New York, New York

Hawkins, Alan J.Tamara A. Fackrell (editors) (2009) *Should I Keep Trying to Work it Out? A Guidebook for Individuals and Couples at the Crossroads of Divorce (and Before).* Utah Commission on Marriage, Salt Lake City, UT.

House, H. Wayne Ed, (1990). *Divorce and Remarriage: Four Christian Views,* Inter-Varsity Press, Downers Grove, IL.

Instone-Brewer, David (2002). *Divorce and Remarriage in the Bible, The Social and Literary Context,* William B. Eerdmans Publishing Company, Grand Rapids, MI.

Instone-Brewer, David (2003). *Divorce and Remarriage in the Church, Biblical Solutions for Pastoral Realities.* Intervarsity Press, Downers Grove, Illinois 60515-1426

Keener, S., (2007) *...and Marries Another: Divorce and Remarriage in the Teachings of the New Testament,* Hendrickson Publishers, Inc. P. O. Box 3473, Peabody, MA 01961-3473.

Kostenberger, Andreas J. (2004).*God, Marriage and the Family: Rebuilding Biblical Foundations,* Crossway Books, Wheaton, IL.

Layfield, Lavelle, (2003) *When Marriages Bomb there is a Balm in Jesus Christg,* LayMar Publishers, 111 Penny Lane, Athens, TX 75751-3247.

Lowery, Fred, (2002) *Covenant Marriage: Staying Together for Life,* Howard Books, 1230 Avenue of the Americas, New York, NY 10020.

MacArthur, John (2009) *The Divorce Dilemma,*Day One Christian Ministries, Inc. Greenville, NC.

Murray, John, (1961). *Divorce,* Presbyterian and Reformed Publishing Co. Phillipsburg, NJ.

Schubert, Joe D. (1966). *Marriage, Divorce and Purity.* Biblical

Research Press, 774 East North 15th Street, Abilene, Texas 79601.

Shelly, Rubel, (2007). *Divorce and Remarriage: A Redemptive Theology.* Leafwood Publishers, Abilene, TX.

Showers, Renald E., (1983) *Lawfully wedded: What constitutes marriage in the sight of God?* Philadelphia College of the Bible, p.36

Smoke, Jim (1995). *Growing Through Divorce,* Harvest House Publishers, Eugene, OR.

Spencer, William & Aida, Tracy, Steve & Celestia, (2009), *Marriage at the Crossroads,* Inter-Varsity Press, P. O. Box 1400, Downers Grove, IL 60515-142.

Strauss, Mark L., Gordon J. Wenham, William A. Heth, and Craig S. Keener (2006). *Remarriage After Divorce in Today's Church: Three Views,* Zondervan, Grand Rapids, MI.

Thomas, Gary, (2000) *Sacred Marriage.* Zondervan, Grand Rapids, MI.

Thomas, J. D. (1977). *Divorce and Remarriage,* Biblical Research Press, 774 East North 15th St, Abilene, TX 79601.

Waldron, Jim, (1977). *Divorce Debate between Olan Hicks and Jim Waldron,* J. C. Choate Publications, Winona, Ms.

Gresham R. Holton

Christians Single, *Again*

www.ingramcontent.com/pod-product-compliance
Lightning Source LLC
LaVergne TN
LVHW011225080426
835509LV00005B/332